# All of Grace

### in Modern English

An Earnest Word with Those Who Are Seeking Salvation
by the Lord Jesus Christ

"Where sin increased, grace abounded all the more."
(Romans 5:20)

## by *Charles Haddon Spurgeon*
*updated & revised by Roger McReynolds*

**Abbreviations**

NASB—The New American Standard Bible

ACKNOWLEDGEMENTS
Proofreaders: Laura Rooke & Patti McReynolds
Cover and formatting: AmberSmartDesigns     Cover photo: Zee Smart

ALSO UPDATED INTO MODERN ENGLISH (and using the ESV)

## Charles Haddon Spurgeon

*According to Promise: The Lord's Method of Dealing with His Chosen People*

*All of Grace*

*All of Grace* (in Large Print 16-point font)

*John Ploughman's Everyday Advice*

*John Ploughman's Talk*

*Lectures to My Students Volume One*

*Matthew The Gospel of the Kingdom Expanded*

*Most Things Spurgeon:* A One Year Daily Devotional

*Peace and Purpose in Trial and Suffering*

*Spurgeon's Catechism:* With Proof Texts in the English Standard Version

*Spurgeon's Commentary on Psalms 1-57*

*The Clue of the Maze: 70 Daily Readings for Conquering Doubt* + 3 Sermons on Doubting

*The Imprecatory Psalms from Spurgeon's The Treasury of David*

*The New Spurgeon's Devotional Bible:* A 600,000 Word Two Year Devotional

*The Penitential Psalms from Spurgeon's The Treasury of David*

*The Soul Winner*

### Spurgeon's Sermons Series

*3:16*: Thirteen Selected Sermons

*A Defense of Calvinism:* Including 7 Sermons on the Doctrines of Grace

*A Sower Went Out to Sow: Nine Sermons on The Parable of the Sower*

*Lost and Found*: Ten Evangelistic Sermons

*The Prodigal Son and Other Parables of Jesus*

## Other Works

*Sermons of D. L. Moody: 21 Sermons*

*The Fear of God*, by John Bunyan

*The Reformed Pastor*, by Richard Baxter

# Table of Contents

# CHAPTER ONE

# To You the Reader

I will be greatly disappointed if this book does not lead many to the Lord Jesus. It is written in childlike dependence in the power of God the Holy Spirit to use it for the conversion of millions, if he so pleases. No doubt many, who pick up this little book, will not have the higher education of others, and the Lord will visit them with his grace. To make sure of this, I have used the clearest language and many common illustrations. But if those with many letters after their names should glance at this book, the Holy Spirit can influence them also. After all, something that can be understood by the less educated should not be difficult for the most scholarly people. Perhaps some might read it who will become great winners of souls for the Lord Jesus Christ!

Who knows how many will find their way to peace by what they read here? A more important question to you, dear reader, is this: Will you be one of them?

A certain man built a fountain by the side of the road and he hung a cup near it with a little chain. After it had been there for a while, he was told that a great art critic had criticized the design of the fountain. "But," the man said, "do many thirsty people drink from it?" They told him that thousands of poor people, men, women, and children quenched their thirst at this fountain. Then he smiled and said that he was not bothered by the critic's comment. He only hoped that on some very hot summer's day the critic himself might fill the cup, and be refreshed, and praise the name of the Lord.

So here is my fountain and here is my cup. Find fault if you want to, but please do drink from the water of life. That is all I care about. I would rather bless the soul of what the world thinks is the most insignificant person, than please a famous person and fail to convert them to God.

Reader, are you serious in reading these pages? If you are, then we are in agreement. I am serious in writing them. My goal is that you will find Christ and heaven. Let us seek this together!  I have dedicated this little book with prayer. Will you join me by looking up to God and asking him to bless you while you read? God has seen to it that you have come across these pages and you have a little spare time to read them. Will you give your attention to them? It is a good sign if you will. Who knows but that this will be a blessing for you? At any rate, the Holy Spirit says, "Today, if you hear his voice, do not harden your hearts."

# CHAPTER TWO

# What Are We Up To?

I heard a story. A pastor called on a poor woman, intending to give her help, because he knew that she was very poor. He knocked at the door, with his money in hand, but she did not answer. He assumed she was not at home and went his way. Later, he met her at the church and told her that he had remembered her need. "I called at your house, and knocked several times, and I assumed you were not at home, because there was no answer." "What time did you call, pastor?" "It was about noon." "Oh, dear," she said, "I heard you, pastor. I am so sorry I did not answer, but I thought it was the landlord calling for the rent." Many who do not have enough money to pay their bills know what I am talking about. Now, it is my desire to be heard, so let me say that I am not calling for the rent. That is not my reason for writing this book. I am not writing to ask you for anything, but to tell you that salvation is all of grace. That means it is free, without charge, for nothing!

Often, when we are anxious to win your attention, our hearer thinks, "Ah! Now I am going to be told I am supposed to keep God's laws. It is someone calling to tell me what God demands of me and I am sure I have nothing with which to pay them. I will pretend I am not at home." No, this book does not come to make demands on you, but to bring you something. We are not going to talk about law, and duty, and punishment, but about love, and goodness, and forgiveness, and mercy, and eternal life.

Do not act like you are not at home. Do not turn a deaf ear or a careless heart. I am not asking anything from you in the name of God or others. It is not my intention to require anything from you. I come in God's name to bring you a free gift, a gift that will bring you joy now and for eternity. Open the door and let my pleadings come in. The Lord himself invites you to a conference about your immediate and endless happiness. He says, "Come now, let us reason together." He would not have said this if he did not have your best interests at heart. Do not refuse the Lord Jesus who knocks at your door. He knocks with a hand that was nailed to the cross for people like you. His only purpose is for your good, so favor him with your attention and come to him. Listen carefully and let the good word sink into your soul. Perhaps this is the hour that you will enter into that new life which is the beginning of heaven. Faith comes by hearing and reading is a sort of hearing. Faith may come to you while you are reading this book. Why not! Oh, blessed Spirit of all grace, make it happen!

# CHAPTER THREE

# God Justifies the Ungodly

This message is for you. You will find it in the Apostle Paul's Letter to the Romans, in the fourth chapter and the fifth verse:

"To the one who does not work but believes in him who justifies the ungodly, his faith is counted as righteousness."

I call your attention to those words, "Him who justifies the ungodly." To me, these seem to be very wonderful words.

Are you surprised that the Bible has an expression like that? God "justifies the ungodly." He makes those who are guilty innocent. He forgives those who deserve to be punished. He favors those who deserve no favor. You thought, did you not, that salvation was for good people? That God's grace was for the pure and holy, for those who are free from sin? It has occurred to you that if you were excellent, then God would reward you. And you have thought that because you are not worthy, that there is no way you could enjoy God's favor. You must be somewhat surprised to read a passage like this: "Him who justifies the ungodly." I do not wonder that you are surprised, because, as familiar as I am with the great grace of God, I never cease to wonder at it.

It does sound surprising, does it not, that it is possible for a holy God to justify an unholy person? Our hearts naturally tend to think in a legalistic way. We are always talking about our own goodness and our own worthiness, and stubbornly believe that we must somehow measure up if we expect to win God's notice. Now, God, who sees through all the ways we deceive ourselves, knows that there is no goodness whatever in any of us. He says, "None is righteous, no, not one." He knows that "all our righteous deeds are like a polluted garment." The Lord Jesus did not come into the world to find goodness and righteousness. He came to give them to people who have none. He does not come because we are innocent, but to make us innocent. He justifies the ungodly.

When an attorney comes into court, if they are an honest person, they want to plead the case of an innocent person and justify them before the court. They want to prove that the charges against their client are false. The lawyer's goal should be to justify the innocent person and they should not attempt to shield the guilty party. No human being has the right, and they should not have the power, to justify the guilty. This is a miracle that is reserved for the Lord alone.

God, the infinite and fair Sovereign, knows that there is not a righteous person on the earth that does good and does not sin. Therefore, in the infinite sovereignty of his divine nature and in the splendor of his inexpressible love, he takes on the job of justifying the ungodly. God has come up with the ways and means of making the ungodly person able to stand before him as innocent. He has worked out a system with perfect justice. He can treat the guilty as if they had been completely free of sin their entire life. He justifies the ungodly.

Jesus Christ came into the world to save *sinners*. That is a very surprising thing. And the people who are most amazed by it are those who enjoy his salvation. I know that to me, even after all these years, that this is the greatest wonder I have ever heard, that God would ever justify *me*. I feel like I am a lump of unworthiness, a mass of corruption, and a heap of sin, apart from his almighty love. God has assured me that I am justified by faith that is in Christ Jesus and treated as if I have always been perfect and righteous. He has made me an heir of God and a joint heir with Christ and yet by nature I know I must be counted among the most sinful. I, who am completely undeserving, am treated as if I had been deserving. I am loved with as much love as if I had always been a godly person, where in truth I was ungodly. Who can help being amazed at this? Gratitude for such favor stands in awe and wonder.

Now, while this is very surprising, I want you to notice how available it makes the gospel to you and to me. If God justifies the *ungodly*, then, dear friend, he can justify *you*. Does this not describe you? If you are unconverted at this moment, then it is a very proper description of you. You have lived without God. You have been the reverse of godly. In one word, you have been and are *ungodly*. Perhaps you have not even attended a place of worship on Sunday, but have ignored God's day, and his house, and his Word. This proves that you have been ungodly. Sadder still, it may be you have even tried to doubt God's existence and even gone so far as to say that you did so. You have lived on this beautiful planet, which is full of proof that God does exist, and all the while you have shut your eyes to the clear evidences of his power and Godhead. You have lived as if there were no God. In fact, you would have been very pleased if you could have demonstrated to yourself to a certainty that there was no God whatever. Possibly you have lived many years in this way and now you are pretty well settled in your ways, and yet God is not in any of them. If you were labeled

UNGODLY

it would describe you as accurately as if the sea were to be labeled *salt water*. Would it not?

Perhaps you fall into another category. Maybe you have attended regularly to all the outward forms of religion and yet you have not had your heart in any of them. That would also label you, Ungodly. You have met with the people of God, but never met with God personally. You may have been in the choir, but never praised the Lord with your heart. You have lived without any love to God in your heart or considered his commands in your life. Well, you are just the kind of person to whom this gospel is sent, this gospel that says God justifies *the ungodly*. It is a wonderful gospel, and, happily, it is available for you. It just suits you, does it not? How I wish that you would accept it! If you are a sensible person, you will see this as the remarkable grace of God making a provision for people just like yourself. You will say to yourself, "Justify the ungodly! Why, then why should I not be justified, and justified right now?"

Now, notice further, that for God to provide salvation for those who do not deserve it and have made no preparation for it, makes perfect sense. The only people who need justifying are those who have no justification of their own. Therefore it is reasonable to find a statement like this in the Bible. If any of my readers are perfectly righteous, they do not need to be justified. If you feel that you are doing your duty well and almost putting heaven under an obligation to accept you, then what do you want with justification? What do you want with a Savior or with mercy? You will be tired of my book by this time, because it will have no interest to you.

If any of you are giving yourselves such a proud pat on the back, please listen to me for a little while. As sure as you are alive, you will be lost. You righteous people, those of you whose righteousness all depends on your own good works, you are either deceivers or deceived. The Scripture cannot lie and it clearly says, "None is righteous, no, not one." In any case, I do not have a gospel to preach to the self-righteous. Jesus said he did not come to call the righteous and I am not going to do what he did not do.

If I did call you, you would not come, so I will not call you if you think you are already righteous through your own effort. No, I would ask you to look at that righteousness of yours until you see what a delusion it is. It is not even half as strong as a cobweb. Abandon it! Flee from it! Oh, believe that the only people who are offered justification from God are those who need it. They need something to be done for them so they will be pronounced "Not guilty" when they stand before the judgment seat of God. Depend on it; the Lord only does what is necessary. Infinite wisdom never attempts that which is not needed. Jesus never takes on a job that is unnecessary. To make someone righteous who is already righteous is not work for God— that would be work for a fool. But to make someone righteous who is unrighteous—that is work for infinite love and mercy. To justify the ungodly—this is a miracle worthy of a God. Just so, and he has done it!

Now, look. If a doctor has discovered an effective and certain cure for a disease, where in this world would that doctor be sent? Would he be sent to those who are perfectly healthy? I do not think so. If he was sent to a place where no one is sick, he would feel out of place. There is nothing for him to do. "Those who are well have no need of a physician, but those who are sick." Is it not just as obvious that the great answers of grace and redemption are for those who are soul sick? They cannot be for the healthy, because they would be of no use to them.

If you, dear friend, feel that you are spiritually sick, the Great Physician has come into this world for you. If you are doomed because of your sin, then you are the very person for whom the plan of salvation was designed. The Lord of love had people like you in his mind when he arranged the method of grace.

Suppose someone with a generous spirit decided to forgive everyone who owed them money. It is clear that this only applied to those in their debt. One person owes them $50,000.00, another owes them $2,500.00. Each one has their promissory note stamped PAID and the debt is wiped out. But even the most generous person cannot forgive the debts of those who do not owe them anything. Even God himself cannot forgive sin where there is no sin. Therefore, pardon cannot be for you who have no sin. Pardon must be for the guilty. Forgiveness must be for the sinful. It would be ridiculous to talk about forgiving those who do not need forgiveness or pardoning someone who has never offended.

Do you think you must be lost forever because you are a sinner? This is the very reason why you can be saved. Because you acknowledge that you are a sinner, I would encourage you to believe that grace is available for people just like you. The hymn writer, Joseph Hart, even dared to say:

> "A sinner is a sacred thing;
> The Holy Spirit has made them so."

It is true! Jesus "came to seek and to save the lost." He died and made a real atonement for real sinners. Some people call themselves "miserable sinners," but they really do not mean it. But when I meet with those who say it and sincerely believe it, I feel overjoyed to meet them. I would be glad to talk all night to genuine sinners. The hotel of mercy never closes its doors on people like that. It is open every hour of the day and every day of the week. Our Lord Jesus did not die for imaginary sins. His heart's blood was spilled to wash out deep crimson stains that nothing else can remove.

The person who understands they are a filthy sinner is the very type of person Jesus Christ came to make clean. A gospel preacher once preached a sermon from, "Even now the axe is laid to the root of the trees." After his sermon, one of his hearers said to him, "One would have thought that you had been preaching to criminals. Your sermon should have been delivered in the county jail." "Oh, no," said the good man, "if I were preaching in the county jail, I would not preach from that text. There I would preach, 'The saying is trustworthy and deserving of full acceptance, that Christ Jesus came into the world to save sinners.'" We agree. The law is for the self-righteous, to humble their pride. The gospel is for the lost, to remove their despair.

If you are convinced you are not lost, why would you want a Savior? Would the shepherd go after sheep that never went astray? Why would a woman clean her house looking for money that she knew was in her purse? No. Medicine is for those who are sick, raising to life is for those who are dead, liberation is for those imprisoned, and giving sight is for those who are blind. How can the Savior, and his death on the cross, and the gospel of pardon, be explained unless we assume that people are guilty and worthy of condemnation? The sinner is the reason the gospel exists. You, my friend, who are reading this right now, if you are undeserving, ill-deserving, hell-deserving, you are the type of person the gospel is for. You are the kind of individual for whom the gospel is decreed, designed, and proclaimed. God justifies the ungodly.

I want to make this clear. I hope I have already done so. But still, as clear as it is, only the Lord can make a person see it. When a person first realizes there really is a salvation for sinners, they find it most amazing that this salvation could be for someone as lost and guilty as themselves. They think they must have great sorrow over their sinful life and change their ways. They forget that their sorrow is actually part of their salvation. But, "Oh," they say, "I must be this and that." That is true, but it comes as a result of salvation, not as the cause of it. Salvation comes first, then the results. In fact, salvation comes when they can only be described by the hateful, beggarly, despicable, disgusting name, "Ungodly." That is all a person is when God's gospel comes to justify them.

Therefore, any of you who have nothing to recommend you to God, who are afraid because you do not feel good about yourself or think there must be something good within you before God will accept you; I urge you to firmly believe that our gracious God is both able and willing to accept you without anything to recommend you and to cheerfully forgive you, not because you are good, but because *he* is good.

Does God not make his sun to shine on the evil as well as on the good? Does he not give fruitful seasons and send the rain and the sunshine on the most ungodly nations? Yes, even Sodom had its sun and Gomorrah had its rain. Oh friend, the great grace of God is greater than I can imagine or you can imagine. It deserves your attention and respect! As the heavens are higher than the earth, so are God's thoughts higher than our thoughts. God can pardon more than we can imagine. Jesus Christ came into the world to save sinners. Forgiveness is for the guilty.

Do not attempt to touch yourself up and make yourself something that you are really not. Come to the God who justifies the ungodly just as they are. A great artist was commissioned to paint the people who made the city work. For historic reasons, he wanted to include certain well-known people of the town in his picture. One person to be included was a handyman who was known to everyone in the town. He was always seen around the city wearing his filthy, untidy, worn-out clothes, begging for odd jobs, but he must be included. The artist said to this ragged and rugged individual, "I will pay you well if you will come down to my studio and let me paint your likeness." He came around in the morning, but he was soon sent out the door, because he had washed his face, and combed his hair, and was wearing a respectable suit of clothes. He was needed as a beggar and was not invited in any other position. In the same way, the gospel will receive you into its house if you come as a sinner and no other way. Do not wait till you have reformed your ways. Come now and come as you are for salvation. God justifies *the ungodly*. God takes you where you are right now, in your worst condition.

Come in your filthy worn out clothes. I mean, come to your heavenly Father in all your sin and sinfulness. Come to Jesus just as you are, diseased, filthy, naked, not fit to live nor fit to die. Come, you who are the very dirt of creation. Come, even though you hardly dare to hope for anything except death. Come, even though despair is overwhelming you and piercing your heart like a horrible nightmare. Come and ask the Lord to justify another ungodly person. Why should he not justify you? Come, because this great mercy of God is meant for people like you.

I put it in the words of the text. I cannot put it more strongly. The Lord God himself is he who graciously says, "God justifies the ungodly." He justifies and treats as justified, those who by nature are ungodly. Is this not a wonderful gospel *for you*? Reader, do not put off considering this matter well.

# CHAPTER FOUR

# It Is God Who Justifies

It is a wonderful thing to be justified before God, to be made righteous in his sight. If we had never broken the laws of God, then we would not have needed God's justification, because we would have been righteous in ourselves. The person who has done things they should all their life, and never done anything that they should not have, is justified by God's law. But you, dear reader, are not this kind of person. I am quite sure of it! You are too honest to pretend to be sinless and therefore you need to be justified.

Now, if you try to justify yourself, you will be simply deceiving yourself. Therefore, do not attempt it. It never helps.

If you ask your friends to justify you, what can they do? Some will speak well of you if you do them small favors, but others will backbite you for less. Their judgment is not worth much.

Our text says, "It is God who justifies," and this is far more important. It is an astonishing fact and one that we should consider carefully. Come and see.

In the first place, *no one except God would ever have thought of justifying those who are guilty.* They have lived in open rebellion to God. They have done evil with both hands. They have gone from bad to worse. They have returned to sin even after they have been burned for it and forced to leave it for a while. They have broken the law and trampled on the gospel. They have refused to listen to declarations of

God's mercy and have persisted in ungodliness. How can they be forgiven and justified? Those who know them say, "They are beyond help. They are hopeless cases."

Even Christians look on them with sorrow rather than with hope. But not God! God, in the richness of his electing grace has chosen some of them before the foundation of the world. He will not rest until he has justified them and blessed them in the Beloved. Is it not written, "Those whom he predestined he also called, and those whom he called he also justified, and those whom he justified he also glorified"? So you see, there are some who the Lord has decided to justify. Why should you and I not be included?

No one except God would ever have thought of justifying *me*. I am a wonder to myself. I have no doubt that the same grace is seen just as much in others. Look at Saul of Tarsus, who later became the apostle Paul. He foamed at the mouth against God's servants. Like a hungry wolf, he hunted the lambs and the sheep right and left. Yet God struck him down on the road to Damascus and changed his heart. He justified him so completely that before long this man became the greatest preacher of justification by faith that ever lived. He must have often marveled that he was justified by faith in Christ Jesus, because he was once a great stickler for salvation by the works of the law. No one except God would have ever thought of justifying a man like Saul the persecutor. But, the Lord God is glorious in grace.

But, even if anyone had thought about justifying the ungodly, *no one except God could have done it.* It is impossible for any person to forgive offenses except the person against whom they have been committed. If someone has greatly injured you, you can forgive them; and I hope you will; but no third person can forgive them for their offense against you. If the wrong is done to you, then the pardon must come from you. If we have sinned against God, it is only God who can forgive, because the sin is against him.

That is why David says, in the fifty-first Psalm, "Against you, you only, have I sinned and done what is evil in your sight." The sin has been against God and only God can put the sin behind him. We owe God a great debt and only our great Creator can pay it, if he chooses to do so. And if he does pay it, it is paid! We have sinned against God and no one except the great God can blot out that sin. Therefore, let us go to him and seek mercy at his hands. Do not be led astray by those who tell us we must confess our sins to some priest or pastor. They have no authorization from the word of God for making such a claim. But even if they were ordained to pronounce forgiveness in God's name, it must still be better to go personally to the great Lord through Jesus Christ and seek and find pardon at his hand. We know that is the right way. Forgiveness by proxy is too risky. You should attend to matters about your soul personally. Do not trust your eternity to another human being.

Only God can justify the ungodly, but *he can do it to perfection.* He throws our sins behind his back. He blots them out. He says that even if they are searched for, they will not be found. Why? There is no other reason for it except his own infinite goodness. He has prepared a glorious way that he can make scarlet sins as white as snow and remove our transgressions as far from us as the east is from the west. He says, "I will remember their sins no more." He goes to the greatest length to make an end of sin. An old, old prophet cried out in amazement, "Who is a God like you, pardoning iniquity and passing over transgression for the remnant of his inheritance? He does not retain his anger forever, because he delights in steadfast love" (Micah 7:18).

We are not talking about justice. We are not talking about God dealing with people according to what they deserve. If you want to deal with the righteous Lord on terms of his law, then everlasting wrath threatens you, because hell is what you deserve. But blessed be his name, he does not deal with us according to our sins. He treats us according to his free grace and infinite compassion. He says, "I will heal their apostasy; I will love them freely, for my anger has turned from them." Believe it, because it is certainly true. The great God is able to treat the guilty with great mercy. He is able to treat the ungodly as if they had always been godly.

Read carefully the parable of the prodigal son in the fifteenth chapter of The Gospel According to Luke. See how the forgiving father received the returning wayward son with as much love as if he had never gone away and had never defiled himself with prostitutes.

The father carried his love so far that the older brother became angry, but the father never withdrew his love. Oh, my brother, my sister, however guilty you may be, if you will only come back to your God and Father, he will treat you as if you had never done wrong! He will regard you as blameless and deal with you accordingly. What do you say about this?

Do you see how wonderful this is? I want to be sure I have made this as clear as possible. No one except God would think of justifying the ungodly, and no one except God could do it, and he has done it! See how the apostle Paul throws out this challenge, "Who shall bring any charge against God's elect? It is God who justifies." If God justifies a person, it is done well, it is done correctly, it is done with justice, and it is done forever.

I read a statement in a magazine that is full of venom against the gospel and those who preach it. The writer says we hold to some kind of theory that we imagine that sin can be removed from people. We hold no such theory. We proclaim it as fact. The grandest fact under heaven is this: Christ, by his precious blood actually puts sin away. And God, for Christ's sake, deals with people with divine mercy, forgives the guilty and justifies them, not according to anything good he sees in them, or sees will be in them in the future, but according to the riches of his mercy that come from his own heart. We have preached this good news, we do preach this good news, and we intend to preach this good news for as long as we live. "It is God who justifies." It is God who justifies the ungodly. He is not ashamed of doing it and we are not ashamed of preaching it.

The justification that comes from God is absolutely final. If the Judge acquits me, who can condemn me? If the highest court in the universe has pronounced me not guilty, who shall bring any charge against me? The conscience that has been made aware of its sinful state is satisfied in knowing that God has justified its case. The Holy Spirit gives our entire nature peace and we are no longer afraid. Our answer to all the shouts and protests of Satan and wicked people is, "God justifies the ungodly." God has justified us and we can now die in peace. God justified us and we will boldly rise again and face the last great judgment.

"Bold shall I stand in that great day,
For who anything to my charge shall lay?
While by my Lord released I am
From sin's tremendous curse and blame."
—Count Zinzendorf

Friend, *the Lord can blot out all your sins*. I am not just guessing when I say, "Every sin and blasphemy will be forgiven people." If you are up to your neck in crime, he can remove the contamination by saying, "I will; be clean." The Lord is a great forgiver.

The Apostle's Creed states, "I believe in the forgiveness of sins." Do you? The Lord Jesus, at this very hour can say, "Your sins are forgiven…go in peace." And if he does this, no power in heaven, or earth, or under the earth, can place you under suspicion, much less under God's wrath. Do not doubt the power of Almighty love. If other people had offended you like you have offended God, you could not forgive them. But you must not measure God's ability to forgive with yours. His thoughts and ways are as much above yours as the heavens are high above the earth.

"Well," you say, "it would be a great miracle if the Lord were to pardon me." Yes, it would be! It would be a supreme miracle and therefore he is likely to do it. He "does great things and unsearchable, marvelous things without number."

I was once afflicted with a horrible sense of guilt. My life was miserable; but then I heard the command, "Turn to me and be saved, all the ends of the earth! For I am God, and there is no other." I turned, and in a moment the Lord justified me. I saw Jesus Christ, made sin for me, and that sight gave me peace. When those who were bitten by the fiery serpents in the wilderness looked to the serpent of bronze they were healed immediately. And so was I when I looked to the crucified Savior.

The Holy Spirit gave me the means to believe and gave me peace through believing. I felt as sure that I was forgiven as I had previously felt I was condemned. I had been certain that I was condemned because the word of God declared it, and my conscience also condemned me. But when the Lord justified me, I became just as certain that I was no longer condemned, by that same word of God and that same conscience. The Bible says, "Whoever believes in him is not condemned," and my conscience believed that God could pardon me and still be fair. So, the Holy Spirit and my own conscience were in agreement. Oh, how I wish that my reader would accept God's word about this. If they would, then their own conscience would soon come to peace in this matter.

I would even dare to say that a sinner justified by God stands on more solid ground that a righteous person justified by their works, if there is such a thing. We could never be sure that we had done enough works. Our conscience would always be uneasy. What, after all, if we come up short. What if what we thought were enough good works turned out to not be enough? What would the Judge of the universe say when we finally ended up in his courtroom?

But when God himself justifies us by his grace and the Holy Spirit gives us peace with God, why then the case is dismissed and we enter into rest. No tongue can describe the depth of that calm that comes over the soul that has received "the peace of God, which surpasses all understanding."

# CHAPTER FIVE

# Just and the Justifier

We have seen that the ungodly can be justified and have considered the great truth that only God can justify anyone. We now come a step further and ask, How can a just God justify a guilty person? Paul gives us the complete answer in the third chapter of his Letter to the Romans. We will read verses 21 through 26:

"But now the righteousness of God has been manifested apart from the law, although the Law and the Prophets bear witness to it—the righteousness of God through faith in Jesus Christ for all who believe. For there is no distinction: for all have sinned and fall short of the glory of God, and are justified by his grace as a gift, through the redemption that is in Christ Jesus, whom God put forward as a propitiation by his blood, to be received by faith. This was to show God's righteousness, because in his divine forbearance he had passed over former sins. It was to show his righteousness at the present time, so that he might be just and the justifier of the one who has faith in Jesus."

Allow me to give you a bit of personal experience. When the Holy Spirit was convicting me of sin, I had a clear and sharp sense of the justice of God. Whatever sin might be to other people, it was an intolerable burden to me. It was not so much that I feared hell, but that I feared sin. I knew that I was so horribly guilty and I remember thinking that if God did not punish me for sin, he should. I felt that the Judge of all the earth should condemn sin such as mine. I sat as my own judge and condemned myself to perish. I acknowledged that if I was God I must sentence such a guilty creature like myself to the lowest hell.

All of this time I was deeply concerned for the honor of God's name and the fairness of his moral code. I felt that my conscience would not be satisfied if I could be forgiven unfairly. The sin I had committed must be punished. But then there was the question of how God could be fair, and yet justify me who had been so guilty. I asked in my heart, "How can God be just and yet the justifier?" The question worried and wearied me, nor could I see any answer to it. I could not invent or imagine an answer that would satisfy my conscience.

To my mind, the doctrine of the atonement is one of the surest proofs of the divine inspiration of Holy Scripture. Who would or could have thought of the just Ruler dying for the unjust rebel? This is no legend dreamed up by someone. No poet's imagination came up with verses creating such a view. This method of making wrongs right is only known among us because it is a fact. Fiction could not have come up with it. God himself decided it. It is not something that could have been imagined.

I had heard the plan of salvation by the sacrifice of Jesus since I was a young boy, but I did not know any more about it deep down in my soul than if I had been born and raised in a remote tribe far away from civilization. The light was there, but I was blind. Only the Lord himself could make the matter plain to me. It came to me as a surprise, as if I had never read in the Bible that Jesus was the answer, and that his sacrifice could make the just God my friend. I believe it will come as a surprise to every newborn child of God whenever they see this truth. I am talking about that glorious teaching that the Lord Jesus came as a substitute. I came to realize that salvation was possible because Jesus sacrificed himself for others. I came to understand that this arrangement for a substitute was made before God created Adam and Eve. I was made to see that Jesus is the Son of God and that he is coequal and coeternal with the Father and that an agreement was made that he would be the Leader of a chosen people, and that as their Leader he would suffer for them and save them.

Our fall did not begin as a personal one. We fell first in Adam who represented all humanity. Therefore, it became possible for us to be recovered by a second representative. And we know that second representative is the Lord Jesus Christ who, as the Leader of his people, volunteered to become the second Adam. I saw that before I had actually sinned I had already fallen by my first father's sin; and I rejoiced when I came to see I could be legally rescued by a second representative.

The fall by Adam left a legal loophole, a way of escape. Another Adam can undo the damage done by the first. I was worried about how a just God could pardon a guilty sinner. Then I understood and saw by faith that the Son of God became a man and in his own blessed person he paid the price of my sin in his own body on the cross. He was pierced for my transgressions; he was crushed for my iniquities; upon him was the chastisement that brought me peace. The wounds inflicted on him healed me.

Dear friend, *have you ever seen that?* Have you ever understood how God can be completely just, how he can dispense the punishment for guilt without holding back at all, and yet can be infinitely merciful and justify the ungodly who turn to him? It was because the supremely glorious and matchless Son of God fulfilled the law by suffering the sentence that I deserved that therefore God is able to pass my sin by. The law of God was more satisfied by the death of Christ than it would have been if all transgressors had been sent to hell. For the Son of God to suffer for sin brings more glory to God than if the whole human race was made to suffer.

Jesus has endured the death penalty in our place. Behold the wonder! There he hangs on the cross! This is the greatest sight you will ever see. Son of God and Son of Man, there he hangs, enduring unimaginable pains, the righteous for the unrighteous, to bring us to God. Oh, the glory of that sight! The innocent is punished! The Holy One is condemned! He who is forever blessed is made a curse! He who is infinitely glorious is put to a shameful death!

The more I look at the sufferings of the Son of God, the more sure I am that they are more than enough to satisfy God with my case. Why did he suffer, unless it was to turn God's wrath away from us? Those who believe in Jesus have no reason to fear it. It must be the case, because God's justice has been satisfied. God can now forgive without needing to change his law or his justice. And our conscience can be at peace. Whatever the wrath of God against iniquity may be, it must be more terrible than we can comprehend. Moses put it well when he asked, "Who considers the power of your anger?" And yet when we hear the Lord of glory cry, "Why have you forsaken me?" and see him yielding up his spirit, we feel that the justice of God has been completely satisfied by the obedience of one so perfect who died such a terrible death. If God himself submits to his own law, what more can be done? There is more value in Christ's death than all human sin can overcome.

The great ocean of Jesus' loving self-sacrifice can swallow up the mountains of our sins, all of them. However unworthy we may be in and of ourselves, the Lord may look on us with favor for the sake of the infinite good of this one representative man. It was a miracle of miracles that the Lord Jesus Christ would stand in our place and endure his Father's righteous anger so that we would not need to. He has done it. "It is finished." God will spare the sinner because he did not spare his Son. God can pay no attention to your sins because he placed those sins on his only Son two thousand years ago. If you believe in Jesus (and that is the point), then your sins were carried away by Jesus who was the scapegoat for his people.

*What is it to believe in Jesus?* It is not merely to say, "He is God and the Savior." It is to trust him completely and absolutely, to take him as the payment for your salvation from this time forth and forever, and take him as your Lord, your Master, your all.

If you will have Jesus, he has you already. If you believe in him, I tell you, you cannot go to hell. That would make Christ's sacrifice ineffective. It cannot be that a sacrifice would be accepted by God and then the person for whom the sacrifice had been offered would then be sentenced to death. If Jesus died in my place, why would I die also? Every believer can claim that the sacrifice was actually made for them. By faith, the believer in Christ has laid their hands on the Lamb of God and made him their own. Therefore, they may rest assured that they can never perish. The Lord would not receive this offering on our behalf and then condemn us to die. The Lord cannot read our pardon written in the blood of his own Son and then punish us. That is impossible. Oh that you may have the grace given you to look right now to Jesus. Begin at the beginning. Jesus is the source of mercy to guilty people!

God justifies the ungodly. "It is God who justifies." That is the only reason it can happen and he does it through the atoning sacrifice of his divine Son. Therefore it can be done fairly, so fairly that no one will ever question it, so thoroughly that in that last great day, when heaven and earth will pass away, there will be no one that will deny the reasonableness of the justification. "Who is to condemn? Christ Jesus is the one who died." "Who shall bring any charge against God's elect? It is God who justifies."

Now, poor soul! Will you come into this lifeboat, just as you are? There is safety here from the sinking wreck! Accept the certain rescue. "I have nothing with me," you say. You are not asked to bring anything with you. People who escape for their lives will leave even their clothes behind. Leap for it, just as you are.

I will tell you this thing about myself to encourage you. My only hope for heaven lies in the full atonement made on Calvary's cross for the ungodly. I rely on that firmly. I do not have the shadow of a hope anywhere else. You are in the same condition as me. Neither of us have anything of our own worth trusting in. Let us join hands and stand together at the foot of the cross and trust our souls once for all to him who shed his blood for the guilty. We will be saved by the same Savior. If you perish trusting him, I must perish also. What more can I do to prove my own confidence in the gospel I am setting before you?

# CHAPTER SIX

# About Being Kept from Sinning

In this chapter I have a few words to those who understand the way of justification by faith that is in Christ Jesus, but have trouble stopping their sinning. We can never be happy, at peace, or spiritually healthy until we become holy. We must be free from sin. But how does this freedom come about? For many, this is the life-or-death question. The old nature is very strong. They have tried to hold it back and tame it, but it will not be conquered. They find that though they are eager to be better, if anything they are growing worse than before. The heart is so hard, the will is so stubborn, the passions are so furious, the thoughts are so unpredictable, the imagination is so uncontrollable, the desires are so wild, that the person feels that they have a den of wild animals living inside of them, that would rather eat them up than be ruled by them.

Our fallen nature seems to be like Leviathan, about whom the Lord said to Job, "Will you play with him as with a bird, or will you put him on a leash for your girls?" A person might as well hope to hold the north wind in the hollow of their hand as expect to control by their own strength those wild powers that live within their fallen nature. This is a greater feat than any the legendary Hercules is claimed to have done. God is needed here.

"I could believe that Jesus would forgive sin," says one, "but then my trouble is that I sin again, and that I feel such awful tendencies within me to sin. A stone thrown up into the air will soon come down again to the ground and I feel like that stone. When I hear wonderful preaching I feel like I am ascending to heaven, but I soon return again to my senseless condition. I am so easily fascinated by the hypnotic eyes of sin and held under a spell that I cannot escape from my own foolishness."

Dear friend, salvation would be a sadly incomplete condition if it did not deal with this part of our fallen life. We want to be made pure as well as be pardoned. Justification without sanctification would not be salvation at all. It would call the leper clean and leave them to die from their disease. It would forgive the rebellion and allow the rebel to remain an enemy to their king. It would remove the consequences of sin, but overlook their cause. It would leave us in a hopeless and desperate situation. It would dam up the stream for a little while, but eventually the polluted lake will break through with more power than ever.

Remember that the Lord Jesus came to take away sin in three ways. He came to remove *the penalty* of sin, *the power* of sin, and finally, *the presence* of sin. You may go from the first to the second immediately. It is not impossible. And then you will be on the road to the third, that is, the removal of the presence of sin. We know "that he appeared to take away sins."

The angel of the Lord said to Joseph that Mary would be his wife and that, "She will bear a son, and you shall call his name Jesus, for he will save his people from their sins." Our Lord Jesus came to destroy the works of the devil that are in us. The same thing that was said at our Lord's birth was also pictured in his death. At the cross, "One of the soldiers pierced his side with a spear, and at once there came out blood and water." This represented the double cure that delivered us from the guilt and the poison of sin.

However, if you are troubled by the power of sin and your tendency to fall into it, as you well may be, here is a promise for you. Have faith in this promise. It is part of the guarantee of grace that God has given and he cannot tell a lie. This promise is found in Ezekiel 36:26:

"I will give you a new heart, and a new spirit I will put within you. And I will remove the heart of stone from your flesh and give you a heart of flesh."

You see, it is all "I will," and "I will." "I will give," and "I will remove." This is the royal way of the King of kings who is able to accomplish everything he wills. No promise of his will ever be broken.

The Lord knows full well that you cannot change your own heart and cannot cleanse your own nature. But he also knows that he can do both. The prophet Jeremiah asked, "Can the Ethiopian change his skin or the leopard his spots?" The answer, of course, is God can. Hear this and be amazed. He can also create you a second time; he can cause you to be born again. This is a miracle of grace, but the Holy Spirit will do it. It would be very amazing if one could stand near the bottom of Niagara Falls, and could speak a word that would make the Niagara River begin to run upstream, and leap up that great cliff over which that river now rolls in stupendous force. Nothing except the power of God could accomplish that marvel! But that would be more than a suitable parallel to what would take place if the course of your nature were completely reversed. All things are possible with God. He can reverse the direction of your desires and the current of your life. Instead of going downward away from God, he can make your whole being tend upward toward God. In fact, that is what the Lord has promised to do for all who are in the covenant and we know from the Bible that all believers are in the covenant. Let me read the words again:

"I will give you a new heart, and a new spirit I will put within you. And I will remove the heart of stone from your flesh and give you a heart of flesh."

What a wonderful promise! In Christ Jesus it is a fact, to the glory of God. Let us grab hold of it; accept it as true and apply it to ourselves. Then it will be fulfilled in us. And in the days and years to come, we will be able to sing about that amazing change that the sovereign grace of God has made in us.

This deserves our consideration. When the Lord removes the heart of stone, that deed is done. And when it is done, no known power can ever take away that new heart that he gives us and that upright spirit that he places within us. "The gifts and the calling of God are irrevocable." God will not and cannot take away what he has once given. Let him breathe new life into you and you will have new life. People reform and clean up their lives, but it soon comes to an end. They are like the proverb that talks about a dog returning to its vomit. But when God puts a new heart into us, that new heart is there forever, and will never harden into stone again. He who made it flesh will keep it flesh. We may rejoice in this and be glad forever; God creates the new heart in the kingdom of his grace.

Let me explain what I am talking about by using a story by that popular preacher of the 18th and 19th centuries, Rowland Hill. I will retell it in my own words to illustrate what our Savior meant when he said, "You must be born again."

Think about a cat. What a clean creature she is! How cleverly she washes herself with her tongue and her paws! It is quite a pretty sight! Have you ever seen a pig do that? No, you never have. It is contrary to its nature. It prefers to wallow in the mud. Go and teach a pig to wash itself and see how unsuccessful your effort will be. It would be a great sanitary improvement if swine would be clean. Teach them to wash and clean themselves as the cat has been doing! It is a useless task. You may use force to wash that pig, but it hurries back to the mud and is soon as dirty as ever. The only way that you can get a pig to wash itself is to transform it into a cat; then it will wash and be clean, but not until then! Suppose that such a change could be made; then what was difficult or impossible is easy enough; from now on the pig will be okay sitting on the rug in your living room.

It is the same way with an ungodly person. You cannot force them to do what a regenerated person would most willingly do. You may teach them and set them a good example, but they cannot learn the art of holiness, because they do not care to. Their nature leads them another way. When the Lord makes someone a new person, then all things look different. The change is so great that I once heard a convert say, "Either all the world is changed, or else I am." The new nature naturally follows after what is right like the old nature wanders after what is wrong. What a blessing to receive such a nature! Only the Holy Spirit can give it.

Did it ever strike you what a wonderful thing it is for the Lord to give someone a new heart and an upright spirit? Perhaps you have seen a lobster that has fought with another lobster and lost one of its claws, and a new claw has grown. That is a remarkable thing; but it is even more remarkable that a human being can have a new heart created within them. It is a miracle beyond the powers of nature.

There is a tree. If you cut off one of its limbs, another one may grow in its place. But can you change the tree? Can you change the life-giving sap? Can you make a fir tree produce apples? You can improve it by grafting a better branch into it and that is the parallel that nature gives us of the work of grace. But to actually change the vital sap of the tree would be a miracle indeed. That genius and mystery of God's power works in everyone who believes in Jesus.

If you yield yourself up to his divine working, the Lord will alter your nature. He will bring your old nature under control and breathe new life into you. Put your trust in the Lord Jesus Christ, and he will remove the heart of stone from your flesh, and he will give you a heart of flesh. Where everything was hard, everything will be tender. Where everything tended downward, everything will rise upward with powerful force. The lion of anger will give way to the lamb of meekness. The raven of uncleanness will flee from the dove of purity. The dreadful serpent of deceit will be crushed under the heel of truth.

I have seen such marvelous changes of moral and spiritual character with my own eyes. I see no case as hopeless. I could, if it were appropriate, point out women who were once immoral who are now as pure as the driven snow; and men who blasphemed who now delight everyone around them by their intense holiness. Thieves are made honest, drunkards sober, liars truthful, and those who mocked Christianity its greatest supporters. Wherever the grace of God has appeared to someone, it has trained that person to deny ungodliness and worldly lusts, and to live soberly, righteously, and godly in this present evil world. And, dear reader, *it will do the same for you.*

"I cannot make this change," someone says. Who said you could? The Scripture that we have quoted does not speak about what you will do, but of what God will do. It is God's promise and it is his responsibility to do what he has said he will. Trust in him to fulfill his word to you and it will be done.

"But how is it to be done?" What business is that of yours? Must the Lord explain his methods before you will believe him? The Holy Spirit does it. The way it is done is a great mystery. The person who made the promise has the responsibility of keeping the promise, and God is equal to the task. God promises this marvelous change and he will most certainly carry it out in everyone who receives Jesus, because he has given them "the right to become the children of God."

Oh, that you would believe it! Oh, that you would do the gracious Lord the justice to believe that he can and will do this for you, even though it would be a great miracle! Oh, that you would believe that God cannot lie! Oh, that you would trust him for a new heart and an upright spirit. He can give them to you! May the Lord give you faith in his promise, faith in his Son, faith in the Holy Spirit, and faith in him, and to him will be the praise and honor and glory forever and ever! Amen.

# CHAPTER SEVEN

# By Grace Through Faith

"By grace you have been saved through faith" (Ephesians 2:8).

Let us turn aside a little so that I may ask my reader to adoringly look on the source of our salvation. It is the grace of God. "By grace you have been saved." It is because God is gracious that people are forgiven, converted, purified, and saved. It is not because of anything in them, or that ever can be in them, that they are saved. It is because of the limitless love, goodness, pity, compassion, mercy and grace of God. Therefore, let us spend some time at this source. Behold the pure river of the water of life, as it flows from the throne of God and of the Lamb!

How immense is the grace of God! Who can measure its width? Who can find the bottom of its depth? Like everything else about God, it is infinite. God is full of love, because "God is love." God is full of goodness; the very name "God" is short for "good." Unlimited goodness and love are part of the very essence of the Godhead. It is because "his steadfast love endures forever" that people are not destroyed; because "his mercies never come to an end" that sinners are brought to him and forgiven.

Remember this; or you may fall into the error of focusing so much on the faith, that is the conduit of salvation, that you forget the grace that is the reservoir and source of that faith. Faith is the work of God's grace in us. "No one can say 'Jesus is the Lord' except in the Holy Spirit." "No one can come to me," says Jesus, "unless the Father who sent me draws him." Faith, which is coming to Christ, is the result of divine drawing. Grace is the first and last moving cause of salvation. As essential as faith is, it is only an important part of the machinery that grace uses. We are saved "through faith," but salvation is "by grace." Shout out those words like the archangel's trumpet: "By grace you have been saved." What glad news for the undeserving!

Faith is the channel or conduit pipe. Grace is the source and the stream. Faith is the aqueduct along which the flood of mercy flows down to refresh the thirsty children of men. It is a great pity when the aqueduct is broken. It is a sad sight to see the many noble aqueducts around Rome that no longer carry water into the city, because the arches are broken and the marvelous structures are in ruins. The aqueduct must be kept intact to carry the water; and, even so, faith must be true and undamaged, leading right up to God and coming right down to us, to be a functional channel of mercy to our souls.

I remind you yet again, that faith is only the channel or aqueduct and not the source. We must not focus on faith so much that we praise it above the divine source of all blessing, which is the grace of God. Never make a Christ out of your faith. Never think of it as if it were the independent source of your salvation. Our new life is found in "looking to Jesus," not in looking to our own faith. "All things are possible for one who believes," but the power is not in the believing, but in the God on whom faith depends. Grace is the powerful engine and faith is the drive chain that moves the soul by the power of that engine. Faith is not righteous because it is morally excellent, but because it grips and hangs on to the righteousness of Jesus Christ. The peace within the soul does not come from thinking about our own faith; it comes to us from Jesus who is our peace. Faith touches the fringe of Jesus' garment and power comes out of him into the soul.

Do you see it, dear friend; the weakness of your faith will not destroy you. A trembling hand may receive a gift of gold. The Lord's salvation can come to us though we have only "faith like a grain of mustard seed." The power is in the grace of God, not in our faith. Great messages can be sent along very thin wires, and the peace-giving witness of the Holy Spirit can reach the heart by a thread-like faith that seems almost unable to carry its own weight. Think more about him to whom you look than of the look itself. You must look away from even your own looking, and see nothing but Jesus, and the grace of God seen in him.

# CHAPTER EIGHT

# What Is Faith?

The Bible says, "By grace you have been saved through faith." What is this faith? There are many descriptions of faith; but almost all the definitions I have met with have made me understand it less than I did before I saw them. There is a story of an uneducated slave who said, when he read this passage, that he would *confound* it; and it is very likely that he did so, though his intention was to *expound* it. We may explain faith until nobody understands it. I hope I will not be guilty of that fault. Faith is the simplest of all things. Perhaps its simplicity is why it is so difficult to explain.

What is faith? It is made up of three things—knowledge, belief, and trust. Knowledge comes first. "How are they to believe in him of whom they have never heard?" I need to be informed about something before I can possibly believe it. "Faith comes from hearing." We must hear first, so that we may know what is to be believed. "Those who know your name put their trust in you." Knowledge is important, because a certain amount of knowledge is essential to faith. "Incline your ear, and come to me; hear, that your soul may live." These are the words of the ancient prophet Isaiah and they are still true today.

Search the Scriptures and learn what the Holy Spirit teaches about Christ and his salvation. Seek to know God because, "Whoever would draw near to God must believe that he exists and that he rewards those who seek him." May the Holy Spirit give you the spirit of knowledge and of the fear of the Lord! Seek to understand the gospel. Know what the good news is, how it talks about free forgiveness, and of a change of heart, of adoption into the family of God, and of countless other blessings. Know especially about Christ Jesus the Son of God, the Savior of men and women, united to us by his human nature, and yet one with God; and thus able to act as the Mediator between God and us, able to be the connecting link between the sinner and the Judge of all the earth. Make it your goal to know more and more about Christ Jesus. Make it your special goal to know all about the sacrifice of Christ, because this is the most essential part of saving faith. God was in Christ restoring peaceful relations between himself and the world and not counting their trespasses against them.

Recognize that Jesus became "a curse for us." He was cursed by God for us! Drink deeply from the doctrine of the substitutionary work of Christ, because that is where the sweetest possible comfort to the guilty children of men is found. The Lord "made him to be sin who knew no sin, so that in him we might become the righteousness of God." Faith begins with knowledge.

After knowledge, the mind goes on to *believe* that these things are true. The soul believes that God is real and that he hears the cries of sincere hearts. It believes that the gospel is from God and that justification by faith is the grand truth that God has revealed, by his Spirit, in these last days more clearly than before. Then the heart truly believes that Jesus is our God and Savior; that he is the Redeemer of people, the Prophet, Priest, and King of his people. All of this is accepted as certain truth, not to be called into question. I pray that you may come to this conclusion at once. Believe that "the blood of Jesus his Son cleanses us from all sin." Get to where you believe it strongly. Believe that his sacrifice is complete and fully accepted by God for sinners. Believe that anyone who believes in Jesus is not condemned. Believe these truths like you believe any other facts. The difference between common faith and saving faith is mainly a matter of where the faith is placed. Believe what God says as you would believe your own father or friend. "If we receive the testimony of men, the testimony of God is greater."

So far you have been advancing toward faith. Only one more ingredient is needed to complete it. That is *trust*. Commit yourself to the merciful God. Place all your hope on his gracious gospel. Trust your soul on the dying and living Savior. Wash away your sins in the atoning blood. Accept Christ's perfect righteousness and all is well. Trust is the essential part of faith. There is no saving faith without it. The Puritans would often use the word "recumbency" to explain faith. It meant leaning on something with all your weight. Lean on Christ with all your weight. It would be an even better illustration if I said fall at full length and lie on the Rock of Ages. Throw yourself on Jesus. Rest in him. Commit yourself to him. That is exercising saving faith. Faith is not something that is blind, because faith begins with knowledge. Faith does not accept unproven theories, because faith believes in facts of which it is certain. Faith is not an impractical thing of dreams, because faith risks everything on the truth of revelation. That is one way of describing what faith is.

Let me try again. Faith is believing that Christ is what he is said to be, that he will do what he has promised to do, and then to expect him to do it. The Bible says that Jesus Christ is God, God in human flesh; it says that his character was perfect, that he became a sin offering on our behalf, and that he himself bore our sins in his body on the cross. The Scripture talks about Christ as having finished transgression, making an end of sin, and bringing in everlasting righteousness. The sacred text goes on to state he "died for our sins," "was raised on the third day," that he "always lives to make intercession for" us, that he has gone up to glory, and has taken possession of heaven on the behalf of his people, and that he will come again soon to "judge the world with righteousness and the peoples with equity." We are to believe these things most firmly, because this is the testimony of God the Father when he said, "This is my beloved Son…listen to him." God the Holy Spirit has also borne witness to Christ, both in the inspired word by many miracles, and by working in the hearts of men and women. We are to believe that the Spirit's testimony is true.

Faith also believes that Christ will do what he has promised. Faith believes Jesus when he promised, "Whoever comes to me I will never cast out." Therefore, faith is certain that Jesus will not throw us out if we come to him. Faith believes that since Jesus said, "The water that I will give him will become in him a spring of water welling up to eternal life," then it must be true; and if we get this living water from Christ it will continue in us, and will well up within us in streams of holy life. Whatever Christ has promised to do he will do. We must believe this and look to him for pardon, justification, preservation, and eternal glory, according to the promises he has made to those who believe in him.

Then comes the next necessary step. Faith believes that Jesus is what the Bible says he is and that Jesus will do what he says he will do. Each individual must trust him to be what he says he is and believe he will do what he has promised to do for everyone who believes in him. Faith places the individual in the hands of Jesus, believing that he has been appointed to save and that he can save those who believe in him. Faith rests on his promise that he will do just what he says he would. This is saving faith and the person who has it has everlasting life. Whatever the dangers and difficulties, whatever the darkness and depression, whatever the weaknesses and sins, the person who believes in Christ Jesus in this way is not condemned, and will never come into condemnation.

I trust this explanation has helped and will be used by the Spirit of God to direct my reader into immediate peace. "Do not fear, only believe." Trust, and be at peace.

My fear is that the reader might be satisfied with understanding what needs to be done and yet never do it. The poorest real faith actually at work in the heart is better than the best understanding that is not acted on. Do not be overly concerned with definitions and fine points. The important thing is to believe in the Lord Jesus at once. A hungry man lives because he eats. He does not need to understand how food is produced, or how the muscles in his mouth work, or the process of digestion; he eats and he lives. Someone else may be far cleverer, and thoroughly understand the science of nutrition, but if they do not eat they will die, even with all their knowledge.

There is no doubt that many who are in hell at this very hour understood the doctrine of faith, but did not believe. On the other hand, not one person who has trusted in the Lord Jesus has ever been cast out, even though they may never have been able to define their faith intelligently. Oh, dear reader, receive the Lord Jesus into your soul and you will live forever! "WHOEVER BELIEVES IN THE SON HAS ETERNAL LIFE."

# CHAPTER NINE

# How Can We Illustrate Faith?

In this chapter I will give you a few illustrations to explain more clearly what faith is. Only the Holy Spirit can make my reader see, but it is my duty and my joy to provide all the light I can, and to pray to the divine Lord to open blind eyes. Oh, that you would pray the same prayer for yourself!

Saving faith has its parallels in the human body.

The *eye* sees. Our eye can bring that which is far away into the mind. We can bring the sun and the far-off stars into the mind by a glance of the eye. And so by trust, we can bring the Lord Jesus near to us; and though he may be far away in heaven, he enters into our heart. Just look to Jesus. The hymn is absolutely true:

> There is life in a look at the Crucified One,
> There is life at this moment for you.

Faith is *the hand* that grips. When our hand takes hold of anything for itself, it does the same thing faith does when it takes hold of Christ and the blessings of his redemption. Faith says, "Jesus is mine." Faith hears about the pardoning blood and cries, "I accept it to pardon *me*." Faith claims that the inheritance of the dying Jesus is hers; and it is hers, because faith is Christ's heir. He has given himself and everything that he has to faith. Oh friend, take that which grace has provided for you. You will not be a thief, because you are the rightful heir and have been given divine permission to receive it. "Let the one who desires take the water of life without price." The one who is allowed to have a treasure simply by taking hold of it will be foolish indeed if they remain poor.

Faith is the *mouth* that feeds on Christ. Before food can nourish us, it must be received into us. Eating and drinking are simple matters. We willingly receive food into our mouth and then give our consent for it to pass down into our stomach where it is absorbed into our body. Paul says, in his Letter to the Romans, that, "The word is near you, in your mouth." So then, all that needs to be done is to swallow it, to allow it to go down into the soul. Oh, that people had an appetite! The person who is hungry and sees food set before them does not need to be taught how to eat. "Give me," said one, "a knife and a fork and a chance." They were fully prepared to do the rest. Certainly, someone who hungers and thirsts for Christ needs only to know that he is given freely, and they will receive him at once. If this is the case with my reader, then let them not hesitate to receive Jesus. They may be sure that they will never be blamed for doing so, because "all who did receive him, who believed in his name, he gave the right to become children of God." He never rejects anyone. He authorizes every one who comes to remain his child forever.

The ways people make their living illustrates faith in many ways. The farmer buries good seed in the earth and expects it not only to live but also to be multiplied. They have faith in the promise, that "seedtime and harvest...shall not cease," and they are rewarded for their faith.

The retailer deposits their money in the bank and places their trust in the honesty and soundness of the bank. They place their capital in the hands of their vendors and feel far more at ease than if they had gold locked it up in a safe.

Sailors trusts themselves to the sea. When they swim, they take their feet from the bottom and rest on the buoyant ocean. They could not swim if they did not completely plunge into the water.

The goldsmith puts precious metal into the fire that seems eager to consume it, but they receive it back again from the furnace purified by the heat.

You cannot turn anywhere in life without seeing faith in action between one person and another, or between someone and natural law. Now, just as we trust in daily life, we are to trust in God as he is revealed in Christ Jesus.

Different people exhibit faith at different levels. Their faith varies according to the amount of their knowledge or growth in grace. Sometimes faith is little more than a simple *clinging* to Christ; a sense of needing to depend and a willingness to do so. They are very much like the limpet, a marine mollusk noted for how tightly it clings to rocks. When you are down at the seaside you will see limpets sticking to the rock. You walk softly up to the rock, you strike the mollusk with a quick blow from your walking stick and off he comes. Try the next limpet in that way. You have given him warning; he heard the blow with which you struck his neighbor, and he clings with all his might. You will never get him off now; not you! Strike, and strike again, but you may just as well break the rock with your wooden stick. Our little friend, the limpet, does not know much, but he clings. He can cling and he has found something to cling to. This is all the knowledge he has and he uses it for his security and salvation. The limpet has life because it clings to the rock and the sinner has life because they cling to Jesus. Thousands of God's people have no more faith than this; they know enough to cling to Jesus with all their heart and soul, and this is enough for peace in this life and safety in eternity. To them, Jesus Christ is a Savior, a strong and mighty Rock, permanent and unchanging. They cling to him for dear life and this clinging saves them. Reader, can you not cling? Do it now!

Faith is seen when someone relies on another's superior knowledge on a subject. This is a higher faith. This faith knows why it is depending on someone else and acts on it. I do not think the limpet knows much about the rock. But as faith grows it becomes more and more intelligent. A blind man trusts himself with his guide because he knows that his friend can see, and, because he trusts him, he walks where his guide leads him. If the poor man is born blind he does not know what sight is; but he knows that there is such a thing as sight, and that his friend possesses it, and therefore he freely puts his hand into the hand of the one who sees, and follows his guidance. "We walk by faith, not by sight." "Blessed are those who have not seen and yet have believed." This is as good an example of faith as there is. We know that Jesus has excellence, and power, and blessing with him, that we do not possess. Therefore, we gladly trust ourselves to him to be to us what we cannot be to ourselves. We trust him like the blind man trusts his guide. He never betrays our confidence; rather, He "became to us wisdom from God, righteousness and sanctification and redemption."

Every child who goes to school has to exercise faith while learning. Their teacher instructs them in geography, and teaches them about the earth, and the existence of certain great cities and empires. The child does not personally know these things are true, but they believe their teacher and the textbooks. That is what you will have to do with Christ if you are to be saved. You must simply know because he tells you, believe because he assures you it is true, and trust yourself with him because he promises you that salvation will be the result.

Almost everything that you and I know has come to us by faith. A scientific discovery has been made and we are sure of it. On what grounds do we believe it? On the authority of certain well-known scientists whose reputations are respected. We have never made or seen their experiments, but we believe what they tell us. You must do the same with regard to Jesus. Because he teaches you certain truths you are to be his disciple and believe his words. Because he has performed certain acts you are to be his follower and trust yourself with him. He is infinitely superior to you and is worthy to be your Master and Lord. If you will receive him and his words you will be saved.

Another and higher form of faith is the faith that *grows out of love.* Why does a child trust their father? The reason why the child trusts their father is because they love him. Blessed and happy are they who have a sweet faith in Jesus that is linked with a deep affection for him, because they have a relaxed confidence in their Lord. These lovers of Jesus are charmed with his character and delighted with his work. They are so carried away by the loving kindness he has shown that they cannot help trusting him, because they admire, revere, and love him so much.

This loving trust in the Savior may be illustrated like this. A woman is the wife of the most skilled physician of the day. She is stricken with a dangerous illness and is struck down by its power. Yet she is wonderfully calm and quiet, because her husband has made this disease his special study, and has healed thousands who were similarly afflicted. She is not troubled in the least, because she feels perfectly safe in the hands of one so dear to her, who has the highest love for her, and the highest skill in treating her condition. Her faith in her husband is reasonable and natural in every way and he is deserving of it. Those who have this kind of faith in Christ are the happiest of believers. There is no physician that can match him. No one can save like he can. We love him and he loves us. Therefore, we place ourselves in his care, accept what he prescribes for us, and do whatever he asks us to do. We feel that nothing can go wrong while he is in charge, because he loves us too much to let us perish, or suffer a single needless pain.

Faith is at the heart of obedience. This may be clearly seen in the business of life. When a captain trusts a pilot to bring their ship safely into port, they steer their vessel according to the pilot's direction. When a traveler trusts a guide to take them over a difficult pass, they follow the path that their guide points out. When a patient believes in a doctor, they carefully follow their prescriptions and directions. Faith that refuses to obey the commands of the Savior is false faith. It will never save the soul. We trust Jesus to save us; he gives us directions how to be saved; we follow those directions and are saved. Dear reader, do not forget this. Trust Jesus and prove your trust by doing whatever he instructs you.

Another degree of faith comes from *tested knowledge*. It is a result of growth in grace. It is the faith that believes Christ because it has spent much time with him. It trusts in him because it has proven him to be absolutely faithful. An old Christian was in the habit of writing T and P in the margin of her Bible whenever she had *tried* and *proven* a promise. How easy it is to trust a tried and proven Savior! You cannot do this yet, but you will be able to eventually. Everything must have a beginning. You will rise to strong faith in due time. This mature faith does not ask for signs and visible reminders, it bravely believes without them.

Look at the faith of the master mariner. I have often been amazed at it. He casts off the line and sails away from the land. For days, weeks, or even months, he never sees another ship or a shoreline; yet on he goes day and night without fear, until one morning he finds himself exactly where he had been steering. How has he found his way over this vast ocean? He has trusted in his compass, his nautical almanac, his telescope, and the heavenly bodies. He obeyed their guidance and, without sighting land, he has steered so accurately that he has entered into port without having to make any corrections. Sailing without sight, as we know it, is a wonderful thing.

It is a happy state to, spiritually, completely leave the shores of sight and feeling, say, "Goodbye" to inward feelings, signs, and so forth. It is glorious to be far out on the ocean of divine love, believing in God, and steering for heaven by the direction of the word of God. "Blessed are those who have not seen and yet have believed." They will be welcomed into the desired port at last and have a safe voyage on the way. Will my reader put their trust in God in Christ Jesus? This is where my joyous confidence is. Brother, sister, come with me, and believe our Father and our Savior. Come at once.

# CHAPTER TEN

# Why Are We Saved by Faith?

Why did God choose to use faith as the way to salvation? This is a common question. "By grace you have been saved through faith," is certainly the teaching of Holy Scripture and the decree of God; but why? Why has faith been chosen rather than hope, or love, or patience?

We must exercise respectful caution while attempting to answer this question. God's ways are not always intended to be understood, nor are we allowed undue liberties in questioning them. We humbly respond by saying that, as far as we can tell, faith has been chosen as the conduit of grace, because it is the most natural way for faith to be given. Suppose that I am about to give a poor man some money. I put it into his hand—why? Well, it would hardly seem right to stick it in his ear or to place it on his foot. The hand seems to have been made on purpose to receive. Think of faith as the hand that accepts grace.

I will try to be very clear. Receiving Christ by faith is an act as simple as a child receiving an apple from you. You hold it out and promise to give them the apple if they come for it. The child believes and therefore receives the apple. It is exactly the same act of faith that deals with eternal salvation. What the child's hand is to the apple, your faith is to the perfect salvation of Christ. The child's hand does not make the apple, nor improve the apple, nor deserve the apple; it only takes it. Faith has been chosen by God to receive salvation, because it does not pretend to create salvation, nor to help in it, but is simply content to humbly receive it. "Faith is the tongue that begs for forgiveness, faith is the hand that receives it, and faith is the eye that sees it; but faith is not the price that pays for it." Faith never claims she is the reason for pardon. Faith understands forgiveness comes only through the blood of Christ. She becomes a good servant to bring the riches of the Lord Jesus to the soul. She acknowledges where forgiveness comes from and claims she is only used to receive the grace that alone saves.

Faith has also been chosen because *it gives all the glory to God.* It is through faith so it can be by grace, and it is by grace so that no one can brag about it. God cannot tolerate pride. He keeps his distance from the proud and he has no desire to come closer to them. He will not give salvation in a way that gives room for pride. The apostle Paul said, "Not a result of works, so that no one may boast." Faith eliminates all boasting. The hand that receives charity does not say, "I should be thanked for accepting this gift." That would be ridiculous. When the hand brings food to the mouth it does not say to the body, "Thank me, because I feed you." The hand does a very simple and very necessary thing, but it never claims glory for itself for what it does. So God chose faith to receive the indescribable gift of his grace, because it cannot claim any credit for what it does. Faith must adore the gracious God who is the giver of all good. Faith places the crown on the head of the Lord Jesus, and therefore the Lord Jesus places the crown on the head of faith, saying, "Your faith has saved you; go in peace."

Next, God chooses faith to bring salvation because *it is a certain way to link people with God.* When someone places their confidence in God, there is a point of connection between them, and that connection guarantees blessing. Faith saves us because it makes us cling to God and so joins us to him. I have often used the following illustration, but I must repeat it, because I cannot think of a better one.

I am told that years ago a boat capsized above Niagara Falls and two men were being carried down the current. Some people on the shore managed to float a rope out to them and both of them grabbed hold. One of them held on tightly and was safely drawn to the bank. But the other man, seeing a great log come floating by, unwisely let go of the rope and clung to the log, as it was the bigger thing of the two, and apparently easier to cling to. Sadly, the log with the man on it went right over the falls, because there was no connection between the log and the shore. The size of the log was no benefit to the man who hung on to it; it needed a connection with the shore to provide safety. So, when someone trusts in their works, or to sacraments, or to anything like that, they will not be saved, because there is no connection between them and Christ. Faith may seem like a thin rope, but it is in the hands of the great God on the shoreline. Infinite power pulls the connecting rope in and saves the person from destruction. Oh, the blessedness of faith, because it unites us to God!

Again, faith is chosen because *it stirs us to action*. Faith is at the root of even the ordinary things we do. I wonder if I would be wrong to say that we never do anything except through some kind of faith. If I walk across my study it is because I believe my legs will carry me. A person eats because they believe food is necessary for living. They go to work because they believe in the value of money. They accept a check because they believe that the bank will honor it. Columbus discovered America because he believed that there was another continent beyond the ocean. And the Pilgrim Fathers colonized the Americas because they believed that God would be with them on those rocky shores.

Most great accomplishments begin with faith. For good or for evil, faith works wonders by the person in whom it lives. In its natural form, faith is a dominating force that is part of all human actions. Possibly the person who makes the most fun of faith is the very person who has the most faith, but uses it for evil. They usually have so much faith that they tend to believe things that would be ridiculous, if they were not so disgraceful. God gives salvation to faith, because by creating faith in us he touches the emotions in us that stir us to action. He has, so to speak, taken possession of the battery and now he can send the holy current to every part of our nature. When we believe in Christ, the heart belongs to God. We are then saved from sin and are moved toward repentance, holiness, zeal, prayer, dedication, and every other gracious thing. What grease is to the wheels, what the balance wheel is to a mechanical clock, what wings are to a bird, what sails are to a sailboat, that is what faith is to all holy duties and service.

If you have faith, all other graces will follow and continue to stay on course.

Faith in Christ also has power because *it is motivated by love*. Faith influences us to love God and draws the heart after the best things. Beyond all question, the person who believes in God will love God. Faith acts on understanding, but it also comes from the heart. "For with the heart one believes and is justified." God gives salvation through faith because it lives next door to the emotions and is closely related to love; and love is the parent and caregiver of every holy feeling and act. Loving God leads to obeying him. Loving God leads to living a holy life. To love God and to love mankind is to be conformed to the image of Christ; this is what salvation is.

And, faith *creates peace and joy*. The person who has faith is calm and peaceful, is glad and joyful, and this is part of preparing us for heaven. God gives faith all heavenly gifts, so that faith will work a life and spirit within us that will be seen in us forever in the higher and better world. Faith provides us with armor for this life and education for the life to come. It equips us to live and to die without fear. It prepares us for both action and suffering. The Lord chooses faith because it is a most suitable method for bringing grace to us and by that means for preparing us for glory.

Faith certainly does for us what nothing else can do. It gives us joy and peace, and causes us to enter into God's rest. Why do people try to be saved by any other way? An old preacher said, "A silly servant is asked to open a door. He sets his shoulder to it and pushes with all his might; but the door does not budge, and he cannot enter, no matter how strong he is. Another servant comes with a key, easily unlocks the door, and easily enters. Those who try to be saved by works are pushing at heaven's gate without success; but faith is the key that opens the gate at once." Reader, will you not use that key? The Lord commands you to believe in his dear Son and therefore you may do so. And in doing so you will live. Is this not the promise of the gospel, "Whoever believes and is baptized will be saved"? (Mark 16:16). How can you object to a way of salvation that honors the mercy and the wisdom of our gracious God?

# CHAPTER ELEVEN

# I Can Do Nothing!

After the anxious heart has accepted the doctrine of the atonement of Christ on the cross and understood the great truth that salvation is through faith in the Lord Jesus, it is often very troubled with a sense of its inability to do that which is good. Many complain, "I can do nothing." They are not making this into an excuse, but every day they feel their inability to act like they know they should. They would if they could. They can honestly say, "I have the desire to do what is right, but not the ability to carry it out."

This feeling seems to make the gospel ineffective. What use is food to someone if they cannot get at it? What help is the river of the water of life if they cannot drink from it? We remember the story of the doctor and the poor woman's child. The wise doctor told the mother that her little one would soon be better if given the proper treatment. It was absolutely necessary that her boy regularly drink the best wine and that he should spend time at one of the famous German spas. This was his advice to a widow who could hardly afford food to eat! Sometimes, to a troubled heart, the simple gospel of "Believe and live," is not, after all, so simple, because it asks the poor sinner to do what he or she cannot do. To someone who has been awakened to their need, but is not fully instructed, there appears to be a missing link. Salvation in Jesus is close, but how can it be reached? The soul has no strength and does not know what to do. The soul is within sight of the city of safety, but cannot enter its gate.

Does the plan of salvation provide for this lack of strength? It does. The work of the Lord is perfect. It begins where we are and asks nothing of us. When the Good Samaritan saw the traveler lying wounded and half dead, he did not tell him to get up and come to him, and climb on the donkey and ride off to the inn. No, "He went to him," and attended to his needs, and "set him on his own animal and brought him to an inn." This is how the Lord Jesus deals with us in our low and miserable condition.

We have seen that God justifies, that he justifies the ungodly, and that he justifies them through faith in the precious blood of Jesus. We will now look at the condition these ungodly ones are in when Jesus works out their salvation. Many who have been awakened to their need of salvation are not only troubled about their sin, but about their moral failures. They have no strength to escape the moral filth into which they have fallen, nor to keep out of it. They moan not only over what they have done, but also over what they cannot do. They feel powerless, helpless, and spiritually lifeless. It may sound odd to say that they feel dead, and yet it is true. In their own opinion, they are incapable of doing anything good. They cannot travel the road to heaven, because their bones are broken. They have no strength. Happily, though, it is written, to show God's love to us, "For while we were still helpless, at the right time Christ died for the ungodly" (Romans 5:6 NASB).

The soul knows it cannot save itself. It knows it must have help. This verse shows us that the Lord Jesus steps in to give that help. It is not written, "While we were relatively weak Christ died for us," or, "While we had only a little strength." The description is absolute and clear. "While we were still helpless." We had no strength whatever that could help in our salvation. Our Lord's words were absolutely true, "Apart from me you can do nothing." I may go even further and remind you about the great love with which the Lord loved us "even when we were dead in our trespasses." To be dead is even more than to be helpless.

The one thing on which the poor strengthless sinner has to fix his or her mind and hold on to is the divine assurance that "at the right time Christ died for the ungodly." This is the only hope. Believe this and all inability will disappear. In the fable of Midas, everything he touched turned into gold. The reality of faith is that everything it touches turns into good. Our needs and weaknesses become blessings when faith touches them.

Let us spend some time dealing with some of the reasons for this lack of strength. To begin with, someone will say, "Sir, I do not seem to have strength to collect my thoughts and keep them focused on those serious things that concern my salvation. A short prayer is almost too much for me. I think part of the reason is that I have never been able concentrate on one thing for very long. Another is probably because of the immoral life I have lived and I am also easily distracted by worrying about how to make ends meet. I do not think I am capable of having those high thoughts that are necessary before a soul can be saved." This is a very common form of sinful weakness. But please know this; yes, you may be helpless on this point, but there are many others like you. They could not carry on a train of consecutive thought to save their lives. Many poor men and women are illiterate and uneducated, and deep thought would be very difficult work for them. They are so halfhearted and superficial by nature that they could no more follow out a long process of argument and reasoning than they could fly. They could never achieve the knowledge of any great mystery even if they spent their entire life in the effort. But you do not need to be discouraged. You do not need to be able to concentrate and work out complex problems to be saved. A simple reliance on Jesus is all that is necessary. Hold on to this one fact: "At the right time Christ died for the ungodly." This truth will not require any deep research or great reasoning, or convincing argument. There it stands: "At the right time Christ died for the ungodly." Focus your mind on that and depend on it.

Let this one great, gracious, glorious fact rest in your spirit until it perfumes all of your thoughts, and makes you rejoice even though you are helpless, seeing that the Lord Jesus has become your strength and your song, yes, he has become your salvation. According to the Bible, it is a known fact that "at the right time Christ died for the ungodly," even "while they were still helpless." You may have heard these words hundreds of times and yet you have never before understood their meaning. There is a cheering aroma about them, is there not?

Jesus did not die for our righteousness, but he died for our sins. He did not come to save us because we were worth saving, but because we were utterly worthless, ruined, and doomed. He did not come to earth for anything that was in us, but solely and only for reasons that came from the depths of his own divine love.

At the right time he died for those whom he describes, not as godly, but as ungodly. He chose the most hopeless word he could to describe us. If you have only a little mind, yet attach it to this truth; a truth that is suitable to the smallest mental capacity, and is able to cheer the heaviest heart. Let this verse lie under your tongue like a sweet morsel, until it dissolves into your heart and flavors all of your thoughts. Then it will not matter if you seem to be as scatterbrained as the scattered autumn leaves. People who have never excelled in science, nor displayed the least original thinking, have nevertheless still been completely able to accept the message of the cross, and have been saved as a result. Why should you not too?

I hear someone else cry, "Oh, sir. My lack of strength is this, I cannot repent enough!" People have curious ideas about what repentance means! Many imagine that so many tears need to be shed, or so many groans must be moaned, or so much despair must be endured. Where do these unreasonable ideas come from? Unbelief and hopelessness are sins, and therefore I do not see how they can be necessary to acceptable repentance. And yet there are many who think they are needed as part of the true Christian experience. They are greatly mistaken. Still, I know what they mean. I used to feel the same way in the days of my darkness. I wanted to repent, but I thought that I could not do it, and yet all the time I was actually repenting. Odd as it may sound, I felt that I could not feel. I used to get into a corner and weep, because I could not weep. I fell into bitter sorrow, because I could not sorrow for sin. What a mess we make when, in our unbelieving state of mind, we begin to judge our own condition! My heart was failing me for fear, because I thought that my heart was as hard as solid rock. My heart was broken to think that it would not break. I see now that I was displaying the very thing that I thought I did not have, but at the time I did not know what I was doing.

Oh how I wish I could help others into the light that I now enjoy! I would be glad to say a word that might shorten the time they are bewildered and confused. I will say a few plain words and pray that "the Helper, the Holy Spirit," will apply them to their hearts.

Remember this. The person who truly repents is never satisfied with their own repentance. We can no more repent perfectly than we can live perfectly. However pure our tears of sorrow, there will always be some dirt in them. There will always be something to be repented of even in our best repentance. But listen! To repent means to change your mind about sin, and Christ, and the wonderful things about God. There is sorrow implied in repentance, but the main thing is the turning of the heart from sin to Christ. If there is this turning, then you have the essence of true repentance, even if no fear or discouragement should ever cast their shadow on your mind.

If you cannot repent like you think you should, it will help you greatly if you firmly believe that "at the right time Christ died for the ungodly." Think about this again and again. How can you continue to be unfeeling when you know that "Christ died for the ungodly" out of supreme love? Let me persuade you to reason with yourself like this: "Ungodly as I am, though this heart of steel will not change, though I beat my chest in vain, yet Jesus died for people like me, because he died for the ungodly. Oh, that I may believe this and feel the power of it on my hard heart!"

Blot out every other thought from your soul, and sit down and think about this long and hard. Meditate on this one spectacular display of undeserved, unexpected, unparalleled love. "Christ died for the ungodly." Read over carefully the story of the Lord's death as you find it in the four gospels in the New Testament. If anything can melt your stubborn heart, it will be a sight of the sufferings of Jesus and serious thinking about how he suffered all of this for his enemies.

> "Oh Jesus! sweet the tear I shed,
>     While at your feet I kneel,
> Gaze on your wounded, fainting head,
>     And all your sorrows feel.
>
> "My heart dissolves to see You bleed,

This heart so hard before;
I hear You for the guilty plead,
And grief overflows the more.

"'Twas for the sinful that You died,
And I a sinner stand:
Convinced by Your expiring eye,
Slain by Your pierced hand."

—Ray Palmer

Moses struck the rock in the wilderness with his staff and water gushed out. Surely the cross is that wonderworking staff that brings the water of life out of the heart of rock. If you fully understand the meaning of the holy sacrifice of Jesus, you must repent of ever having opposed the one who is so full of love. It is written, "When they look on me, on him whom they have pierced, they shall mourn for him, as one mourns for an only child, and weep bitterly over him, as one weeps over a firstborn." Repentance will not make you see Christ, but seeing Christ will give you repentance. You may not make a Christ out of your repentance, but you must look to Christ for repentance. The Holy Spirit, by turning us to Christ, turns us from sin. Repentance is the effect, Christ is the cause. So look away from your repenting to the cause of your repenting. Look to the Lord Jesus, who should be praised for giving repentance.

I have heard someone else say, "I am tormented with horrible thoughts. Wherever I go, blasphemies creep into my thinking. Frequently, when I am at my work, a terrible suggestion forces itself upon me. And even at night in my bed I am startled from my sleep by whispers of the evil one. I cannot get away from this horrible temptation." Friend, I know what you mean. I have been hunted by this wolf myself. A person might as well hope to fight a swarm of flies with a sword as to control their own thoughts when the devil is on the attack.

A poor tempted soul, who is being assaulted by satanic suggestions, is like a traveler I have read about. A swarm of angry bees attacked him. They were everywhere, his head, ears; his whole body was covered by them. He could not keep them off nor escape from them. They stung him everywhere and threatened to be the death of him. I am not surprised that you feel you are without strength to stop these hideous and disgusting thoughts that Satan pours into your soul. But still, I would remind you of the Scripture before us. "For while we were still helpless, at the right time Christ died for the ungodly."

Jesus knew where we were and where we would be. He saw that we could not overcome the prince of the power of the air. He knew Satan would gnaw at us. But even then, even when he saw us in that condition, Christ died for the ungodly. Cast the anchor of your faith on this! The devil himself cannot tell you that you are godly; so, believe that Jesus died even for people like you. When Satan accused Martin Luther, the reformer would use the devil's own sword to cut off his head. "Oh," said the devil to Martin Luther, "you are a sinner." "Yes," he said, "and Christ died to save sinners." He struck him with his own sword. Hide in this safe place and stay there: "At the right time Christ died for the ungodly." If you take your stand on that truth, then your blasphemous thoughts that you have been unable to drive away will go away by themselves. Satan will see that it is useless to plague you with them.

These thoughts, if you hate them, are not yours. The devil has placed them in your head. He is responsible for them, not you. If you fight against them, they are no more yours than the swearing and lying of rioters in the street. The devil wants to use these thoughts to drive you to despair, or at least keep you from trusting Jesus. The poor diseased woman could not get to Jesus because of the crowd and you are in much the same condition. These dreadful thoughts rush in and crowd your mind and you cannot get to Jesus. Still, she reached out her finger and touched his garment and she was healed. You must do the same.

Jesus died for those who are guilty of "every sin and blasphemy." Therefore, I am certain he will not refuse those who are the unwilling captives of evil thoughts. Throw yourself on him, thoughts and all, and see if he will not be mighty to save. He can quiet those horrible whisperings of the fiend, or he can empower you to see them in their true light, so that they will not overcome you. In his own way he can and will save you and eventually give you perfect peace. Trust him for this and for everything else.

This supposed lack of power to believe is a sadly bewildering type of inability. We are not strangers to the cry:

> Oh that I could believe,
>> Then all would easy be;
> I would, but cannot Lord, relieve,
>> My help must come from you.

Many remain in the dark for years because they have no power, as they say, to do that which is really relinquishing all power and resting in the power of another, even the Lord Jesus. This whole business of believing is really a very curious thing, because people do not get much help by trying to believe. Believing does not come by trying. If someone were to make a statement about something that happened today, I would not tell him that I would try to believe him. If I believed in the integrity of the person who told me about the incident and said that he saw it, I would accept the statement immediately. If I did not think they were an honest person, I would, of course, not believe them. But there would be no *trying* to believe. Now, when God declares that there is salvation in Christ Jesus, I must either believe him right away or consider him a liar. Obviously you do not need to think about which is the right path in this case. God's word must be true and we are compelled to believe in Jesus without hesitation.

It is possible that you have been trying to believe more than you need to. Do not make it your goal to believe more than is necessary. Be satisfied with having enough faith to believe just this, "While we were still helpless, at the right time Christ died for the ungodly." He laid down his life for people when they still did not believe in him, nor were even able to believe in him. He died for people, not as believers, but as sinners. He came to make these sinners into believers and saints; but when he died for them he viewed them as completely unable to believe in him.

If you take the truth that Christ died for the ungodly and believe it, your faith will save you, and you may go in peace. If you will trust your soul with Jesus, who died for the ungodly, you will be saved. You may not have faith to move mountains, nor do any other wonderful works, but you will have enough faith to be saved. It is not great faith, but true faith, that saves. Salvation is not in the faith, but in Christ in whom the faith trusts. Faith the size of a grain of mustard seed will bring salvation. It is not the amount of faith, but the sincerity of faith, that is important. A person can certainly believe what they know to be true. My friend, you know that what Jesus said is true. Therefore, you can believe in him.

The cross is where faith should focus. And, by the power of the Holy Spirit, the cross is the reason for our faith. Sit down and watch the dying Savior until faith springs up spontaneously in your heart. There is no place like Calvary for creating confidence in Christ. The very air of that sacred hill brings spiritual health to trembling faith. Many have stood there watching and said:

> While I view you, wounded, grieving,
> Breathless on the cursed tree,
> Lord, I feel my heart believing
> That you suffered thus for me.

"Alas!" cries another, "I am helpless because I cannot quit sinning and I know that I cannot go to heaven and take my sins with me." I am glad you realize that, because it is quite true. You must be divorced from your sin or you cannot be married to Christ. Think back to young John Bunyan. He was in a field playing sports one Sunday when this flashed into his mind: "Will you keep your sins and go to hell, or will you give up your sins and go to heaven?" That question brought him to a dead stop. It is the same question that everyone will have to answer, because there is no continuing in sin and going to heaven. It is impossible. You must quit sin or quit hoping for heaven. Do you reply, "Yes I am willing. I have the desire to do what is right, but not the ability to carry it out. Sin masters me. I have no strength to do what is right." If you have no strength, our text is still true, "While we were still helpless, at the right time Christ died for the ungodly"

Can you believe that? However many other things may seem to contradict it, will you believe it? God has said it and it is a fact. It is your only hope, so cling to it with a death-grip. Believe that Jesus died for the ungodly and trust in him. You will soon find the power to kill your sin, but apart from Christ you are dealing with a fully armed strong man who will keep you as his slave forever. Personally, I could never have overcome my own sinfulness. I tried and failed. My readiness to sin was more than I could control until, believing that Christ died for me, I threw my guilty soul on him. That is when I received a conquering source that enabled me to overcome my sinful self. The doctrine of the cross can be used to cut sin to pieces, just as the old warriors used their huge two-handed swords and mowed down their foes at every stroke. There is nothing like placing your faith in the Friend of sinners. It conquers all evil. If Christ has died for me, ungodly as I am, helpless as I am, then I cannot live in sin any longer. I must stir myself to love and serve the Lord who has redeemed me. I can no longer think of evil as unimportant. It killed my best friend. I must be holy for his sake. How can I live in sin when he has died to save me from it?

What a marvelous help it is to know you are helpless to understand and believe that at the right time Christ died for the ungodly. Have you caught the idea yet? For some reason, it is difficult for our darkened, prejudiced, and unbelieving minds to see the essence of the gospel. There have been times, when I have finished preaching, when I have explained the gospel so clearly, that it was plainer than the nose on one's face; and yet I could see that even intelligent hearers have not understood what "Turn to me and be saved" meant. Converts usually say that they did not know the gospel until such and such a day even though they had heard it for years. The gospel has remained hidden, not from lack of explanation, but because it is understood supernaturally. The Holy Spirit is ready to reveal the good news and he will give it to those who ask. And when everything is clearly seen, you will see that the gospel can be summed up in the words, "Christ died for the ungodly."

I hear someone else weeping over their sin and saying: "Oh, sir, my condition seems so hopeless. I hear the word of God on a Sunday and it makes a good impression on me. But during the week I meet with evil companions and my good feelings are all gone. My fellow workers do not believe in anything. They say terrible things and I do not know how to answer them. I am so stunned I do not know how to respond." This person is like Pliable in John Bunyan's *The Pilgrim's Progress*. They are impressionable and easily influenced by others' opinions. I tremble for them. But at the same time, I know their weakness can be overcome by the power of God's grace. The Holy Spirit can cast out the evil spirit of fear of others. He can make the coward brave.

Remember, my poor friend, you must not continue in this undecided condition. Beating yourself up over it will not help. Stand up straight and look at yourself. You were never meant to be like a frog in hiding, in fear of life and afraid to either move or stand still. This is a spiritual matter, but you need to be brave and strong in your everyday life too. I would do many things to please my friends, but I would not risk going to hell just to please them. It may be very well to do this and that for the sake of staying on good terms with people, but it is never worth doing something that would injure your friendship with God. "I know that," you say, "but even though I know it, I am not brave enough to stand for Christ." Well, I have the same verse to quote you: "While we were still helpless, at the right time Christ died for the ungodly."

If Peter were here, he would say, "The Lord Jesus died for me even when I was so weak that the servant girl in the courtyard forced me to lie and swear that I did not know the Lord." Yes, Jesus died for those who left him and fled. Take a firm grip on this truth: "Christ died for the ungodly while they were still helpless." This is your way out of your cowardice. Work this into your soul, "Christ died for me," and soon you will be ready even to die for him. Believe it! Believe that he suffered in your place as your substitute, and endured God's wrath for you. If you believe that fact, you will be forced to feel, "I cannot be ashamed of him who died for me." The person who is fully persuaded of this can meet persecution with fearless courage.

Look at the saints in the age of the martyrs. In the early days of Christianity, when this thought of Christ's great love was sparkling in all its freshness in the church, people were not only ready to die, but they became eager to suffer. They came voluntarily by the hundreds to the judgment seats of the rulers and confessed Christ. I do not say that they were wise to welcome a cruel death, but it does prove my point. A true understanding of the love of Jesus lifts the mind above all fear of what the world can do to us. Why should it not produce the same effect in you? Oh, that it would inspire you right now to join the Lord's side and be his brave follower to the end!

May the Holy Spirit help us to reach this point by faith in the Lord Jesus. Then it will be well with our souls!

# CHAPTER TWELVE

# How Can I Increase My Faith?

How can we increase our faith? To many, this is a very serious question. The say they want to believe, but cannot. A great deal of the advice given on this subject is nonsense. Let us be strictly realistic in how we deal with this issue. We need to use common sense in religion as much as anywhere else. "What do I need to do to believe?" Someone was asked the best way to do a certain simple task. The reply was that the best way to do it was to do it at once. We waste time talking about how to do something when the action is quite simple. The shortest way to believe is to believe. If the Holy Spirit has made you sincere, then you will believe the truth as soon as it is presented to you. You will believe it because it is true. The gospel command is clear; "Believe in the Lord Jesus and you will be saved." It is pointless to evade this by questions and objections. The command is clear. Let it be obeyed.

However, if you still have difficulty believing, take it before God in prayer. Tell the great Father exactly what it is that puzzles you and beg him to solve the question by his Holy Spirit. If I cannot believe a statement in a book, and I can ask the author, I am glad to ask them what they mean. If they are a person of integrity, their explanation will satisfy me. Even more so, the true seeker can ask the Lord about the difficult parts of Scripture and be satisfied. The Lord is willing to make himself known. Go to him and see if it is not so. Go at once to a private place and cry, "Oh Holy Spirit, lead me into the truth! Teach me what I do not know."

Here is something else to help you if faith seems difficult. It is possible that God the Holy Spirit will enable you to believe if you listen frequently and seriously to what you are commanded to believe. We believe many things because we have heard them so often. Do you not find this to be the case in your everyday life? If you hear a thing fifty times a day, you will eventually come to believe it. Some people have even come to believe very doubtful things this way. Therefore, I am not surprised that the good Spirit often blesses the routine of hearing the truth repeatedly and uses it to produce faith in what should be believed. It is written, "Faith comes from hearing." Therefore, hear the gospel preached often. If I sincerely and attentively hear the gospel, then one of these days I will find myself believing what I hear, by the blessed working of the Spirit of God on my mind. Only make sure you are hearing the gospel. Do not be distracted by hearing or reading things that steer you away from the gospel.

However, if that seems like poor advice, I would ask you to seriously consider what others have to say about their belief in Jesus. The Samaritans believed because of what the woman at the well told them about Jesus. We believe many things because we trust what others tell us. I believe the country of Japan exists even though I have never seen it. I believe there is such a place because others have been there. I believe that I will die. I have never died, but there are many people who I once knew who have died and therefore I am convinced that I will also die. The evidence convinces me of that fact. So, listen to those who tell you how they were saved, how they were pardoned, and how their lives were changed. If you will look into it, you will find that somebody just like yourself has been saved. If you have been a thief, you will find that a thief rejoiced to wash away their sin in the fountain of Christ's blood. If you have lived an unhappy life of sexual immorality, you will find that men and women who have fallen in that way have been cleansed and changed. If life seems hopeless, all you need to do is get among God's people, and ask around a little, and you will discover that some of the saints have been just as hopeless as you are, and they will be pleased to tell you how the Lord delivered them.

As you listen to one after another of those who have tried the word of God and proved it, the divine Spirit will lead you to believe. Have you not heard about the man from Africa who was told by the missionary that water sometimes became so hard that a person could walk on it? He declared that he believed many things the missionary had told him, but he would never believe that. When he came to England it happened that on one frosty day he saw the river frozen, but he did not dare to walk on it. He knew the river was deep and he was certain he would be drowned if he went out on it. He could not be persuaded to walk on the frozen water until his friend and many others went on it. Then he was persuaded and trusted himself to go where others had safely gone. So, as you see others who have believed in the Lamb of God, and see their joy and peace, you yourself will be gently led to believe. The experience of others is one of God's ways of helping us to trust in the Savior. You must either believe in Jesus or die. There is no other hope for you except in him.

Here is an even better plan. Ask by whose authority you are commanded to believe. This will be a great help for you to have faith. The authority is not mine. Who could blame you for rejecting it if it was? You are commanded to believe by the authority of God himself. You are told to believe in Jesus Christ and you must not refuse to obey your Maker.

The supervisor of a certain company had often heard the gospel, but he was afraid that he might not be welcomed if he came to Christ. One day his good employer sent him a note at his workplace: "Come to my house right after work." The supervisor appeared at his boss's door and his boss came out and said somewhat roughly, "What do you want, John. Why are you bothering me at this time of night? Work is done. What right do you have to be here?" "Sir," he said, "I had a note from you saying that I was to come here after work." "Do you mean to say that merely because you had a note from me you think you can come to my house and bother me after business hours?" "Well, sir," replied the supervisor, "I do not understand you, but it seems to me that, because you sent for me, I had a right to come."

"Come in, John," his employer said. "I have another message that I want to read to you," and he sat down and read these words: "Come to me, all who labor and are heavy laden, and I will give you rest." "Do you think that after such a message from Christ that you can be wrong in coming to him?" The supervisor suddenly saw it, and believed in the Lord Jesus to eternal life, because he recognized that he had good grounds and authority for believing. So do you, poor soul! You have good authority for coming to Christ, for the Lord himself has ordered you to trust him.

If this does not produce faith in you, think about what it is you are to believe. You are told to believe that the Lord Jesus Christ suffered in the place and role of sinners and is able to save all who trust him. Why, this is the most wonderful fact that anyone has ever been told to believe. It is the most fitting, the most comforting, and the most divine truth that was ever set before mortal minds. I urge you to think about it a lot and discover the grace and love contained in it. Study the four Evangelists; Matthew, Mark, Luke and John. Study Paul's letters. See if the message is not so convincing that you are forced to believe it.

If that does not do it, then think about the person of Jesus Christ. Think of who he is, and what he did, and where he is, and what he is. How can you doubt him? He has done nothing to deserve your distrust. Quite the opposite! It should be easy to rely on him. Why crucify him once again by unbelief? To doubt Jesus is to crown him again with thorns and to spit on him again. What! Not trust him? What worse insult did the soldiers at the foot of the cross pour on him than this? They made him a martyr, but you make him a liar. This is far worse. Do not ask, "How can I believe?" Ask a different question. Ask, "How can I disbelieve?"

If none of these things help, then there is something completely wrong about you, and my final word is, submit yourself to God! Intolerance or pride is at the bottom of your unbelief. May the Spirit of God take away your hostility and make you yield. You are a rebel, a proud rebel, and that is why you do not believe your God. Give up your rebellion. Throw down your weapons. Yield to his will. Surrender to your King. I believe that no one ever threw up their hands in self-despair and cried, "Lord, I surrender," but that, before long, faith became easy. The reason you cannot believe is because you still have a quarrel with God, and are determined to have your own will and your own way. Christ said, "How can you believe, when you receive glory from one another?" Pride creates unbelief. Submit to your God. Yield to your Lord. Then you will sweetly believe in your Savior. May the Holy Spirit work in you now, secretly but effectively, and bring you at this very moment to believe in the Lord Jesus! Amen.

# CHAPTER THIRTEEN

# New Life and the Holy Spirit

"You must be born again." To many, these words of our Lord Jesus are like the flaming sword of the angel who guarded the gate to the Garden of Eden. They have given up, because to be born again is beyond anything they can hope to do themselves. The new birth is from above and therefore it is not in the creature's power. Now, I would not think of denying or trying to hide a truth from you, in order to give you a false comfort. I freely admit that the new birth is supernatural and that it is not something the sinner can do for themselves. It would be little help to my reader if I were wicked enough to try to cheer him or her by attempting to persuade them to either reject or forget something that is unquestionably true.

Do you not find it remarkable that in the same chapter where our Lord makes this sweeping declaration that we must be born again, he also clearly states that salvation is through faith? Read the third chapter of John's Gospel and do not stop with the first few verses. It is true that the third verse says:

"Jesus answered him, 'Truly, truly, I say to you, unless one is born again he cannot see the kingdom of God.'"

But then, the fourteenth and fifteenth verses speak:

"And as Moses lifted up the serpent in the wilderness, so must the Son of Man be lifted up, that whoever believes in him may have eternal life."

And the eighteenth verse repeats the same doctrine in the clearest terms:

"Whoever believes in him is not condemned, but whoever does not believe is condemned already, because he has not believed in the name of the only Son of God."

It should be clear to every reader that these two statements must agree, since they came from the same lips, and are recorded on the same inspired page. Why should we attempt to create difficulty where there cannot be any? If one statement assures us something is necessary for salvation that only God can give, and if another statement assures us that the Lord will save us when we believe in Jesus, then we may safely conclude that the Lord will give everything he says is necessary for salvation to those who believe. The Lord creates the new birth in everyone who believes in Jesus. And their believing is the certain evidence that they are born again.

We trust in Jesus for what we are unable to do. If it were in our own power, then why would we need him? It is our job to believe. It is the Lord's job to create new life in us. He will not believe for us and we are not expected to do the work of regeneration for him. It is enough for us to obey the gracious command and see the Lord work the new birth in us. Jesus went so far as to die on the cross for us, he can and will give us all things necessary for our eternal safety.

Someone will say, "But a saving change of heart is the work of the Holy Spirit." This is certainly true. Far be it from us to question or forget it. The work of the Holy Spirit is secret and mysterious and can only be recognized by its results. There are mysteries about our natural birth that it would be wrong to pry into and even more so regarding the holy work of the Spirit of God in our spiritual birth. "The wind blows where it wishes, and you hear its sound, but you do not know where it comes from or where it goes. So it is with everyone who is born of the Spirit." However, we do know this much, the mysterious work of the Holy Spirit cannot be used as an excuse for refusing to believe in Jesus to whom that same Spirit bears witness.

If a man were told to sow a field, he could not refuse by using the excuse that it would be useless to plant unless God caused the seeds to grow. Neither would he be justified in not preparing the soil because only God can create a harvest by his secret ways and supernatural power. The Bible says that, "Unless the LORD builds the house, those who build it labor in vain." But that does not prevent people from going on about their various daily pursuits. No one who believes in Jesus will ever find that the Holy Spirit refuses to work in them. Their believing is the proof that the Spirit is already at work in the heart.

God works, as it were, behind the scenes, but that does not mean that people sit still and do nothing. They go on about their lives without questioning, and yet they could not even move without the divine power giving them life and strength. Their very breath and all their ways are in God's hands. Their power to do anything is given to them by him from day to day. It is the same with grace. We repent and believe, but we could do neither if the Lord did not enable us. We forsake sin and trust in Jesus, but then we look back and realize that it was God who worked in us, "both to will and to work for his good pleasure." It is pointless to pretend that there is any real difficulty about this.

Some truths are hard to explain in words that in actual experience are simple enough. There is no discrepancy between the truth that the sinner believes and that their faith is actually the work of the Holy Spirit. Only a lack of good sense would make people stop and wonder about these things while their souls are in danger. No man would refuse to get into a lifeboat because he did not know the specific gravity of bodies and needed to be absolutely certain of his safety before trusting himself to it. And no starving woman would refuse to eat until she understood the entire process of nutrition. If you, my reader, will not believe until you can understand all mysteries, you will never be saved. If you allow your self-created difficulties to keep you from accepting pardon through your Lord and Savior, you will perish in a condemnation that will be richly deserved. Do not commit spiritual suicide over an enthusiasm for discussing philosophical theories.

# CHAPTER FOURTEEN

# My Redeemer Lives

I have continually spoken to the reader about Christ crucified, who is the great hope of the guilty. But we would be wise to remember that our Lord has risen from the dead and is alive forever.

You are not asked to trust in a dead Jesus, but in one who died for our sins and has risen again for our justification. Jesus is a living friend to whom you may go right now. He is not a mere memory, but a living person who will hear your prayers and answer them. He once laid down his life, but he now lives to carry on the work he began. He is praying for sinners at the right hand of the Father. That is why, "He is able to save to the uttermost those who draw near to God through him." Come and try this living Savior if you have never done so before.

This living Jesus has also been raised to the highest place of glory and power. He no longer works as "the carpenter's son," nor is he troubled by his enemies. He reigns over rulers, and authorities, and above every name that is named. The Father has given him all power in heaven and on earth, and he uses this high gift in carrying out his work of grace. Hear how Peter and the other apostles answered the high priest and the council after they had been arrested and stood before them:

"The God of our fathers raised Jesus, whom you killed by hanging him on a tree. God exalted him at his right hand as Leader and Savior, to give repentance to Israel and forgiveness of sins" (Acts 5:30-31).

The glory that surrounds the resurrected and ascended Lord should breathe hope into every believer. Jesus is not some ordinary, unimportant person. He is "a Savior and defender." He is the crowned and ruling Redeemer of men and women. The sovereign right of life and death is in his hands. The Father has placed all men and women under the peacemaking government of the Son, so that he can give new life to whom he will. He "opens and no one will shut." At his command the soul that is imprisoned by sin and condemnation can be set free in an instant. He stretches out the silver scepter to whoever enters his court so that they may touch it and live.

Sin lives, and the flesh lives, and the devil lives. But Jesus also lives! Whatever power that sin, the flesh and the devil may have to ruin us, Jesus has even greater power to save us!

His position and power are for our benefit. He has been raised up to give. He is happy to be a Prince and a Savior, so that he may give everything that is needed to achieve the salvation of all who come under his rule. Jesus has nothing that he will not use for a sinner's salvation. His superabundant grace is on display when sinners are saved. His kingdom and his Savior-ship are inseparably linked. He would not be satisfied to have one without the other. He is extremely pleased to bring happiness to men and women. They are the finest jewels in the crown of his glory. Could anything be more calculated to raise the hopes of seeking sinners who are looking to Christ?

Jesus endured great humiliation and therefore there was great room for him to be exalted. He humbled himself to endure and accomplish all of the Father's will. He was rewarded for that by being raised to glory. He uses that high position for the benefit of his people. Let my reader raise their eyes to these hills of glory, from where their help must come. Gaze on the high glories of the Prince and Savior. Is it not a most hopeful sign for men and women that a human being now sits on the throne of the universe? Is it not glorious that the Lord of all is the Savior of sinners? We have a Friend at the royal court; yes, even a Friend who sits on the throne. He will use all of his influence for those who entrust their affairs to his hands. Isaac Watts has put it well:

> He ever lives to intercede
>   Before his Father's face;
> Give him, my soul, your cause to plead,
>   Nor doubt the Father's grace.

Come, my friend, and commit your cause and your case to those pierced hands that are now glorified with the royal signet rings of power and honor. No case has ever been lost that was entrusted to the Advocate that we have with the Father, Jesus Christ the righteous.

# CHAPTER FIFTEEN

# Repentance and Forgiveness Go Together

It is clear from the verses we quoted in the last chapter that repentance and the forgiveness of sins are inseparable. In Acts 5:31 we read that God exalted Jesus "to give repentance to Israel and forgiveness of sins." These two blessings come from that sacred hand that was once nailed to the cross, but is now raised to glory. Repentance and forgiveness are welded together by the eternal purpose of God. "What therefore God has joined together, let not man separate."

Repentance must accompany forgiveness. If you think about this a little, you will see how logical this is. It cannot be that pardon of sin should be given to an unrepentant sinner. That would encourage them in their evil ways and teach them that sin is really not all that bad. If the Lord were to say, "You love sin, and you live in sin, and you are going from bad to worse, but, all the same, I forgive you," it would be like issuing a license to sin. The foundations of social order would be removed and moral anarchy would follow. There is no telling how many evil mischiefs would occur if you could divide repentance and forgiveness, and excuse the sin while the sinner remained as fond of it as ever.

Even in our natural world, most people agree that if we continue in our sin, and will not repent of it, we cannot be forgiven but must reap the consequence of our stubbornness. If we believe in the holiness of God, we agree it must also be true on a higher level. According to the infinite goodness of God, we are promised that if we will forsake our sins, confessing them, and will, by faith, accept the grace that is provided in Christ Jesus, God "is faithful and just to forgive us our sins and to cleanse us from all unrighteousness." But as long as God lives, there can be no promise of mercy to those who continue in their evil ways and refuse to acknowledge their wrongdoing. Certainly no rebel can expect the king to pardon their treason while they remain in open rebellion. No one can be so foolish as to imagine that the Judge of all the earth will bury our sins if we refuse to bury them ourselves.

Mercy and sin cannot be in agreement. This must be the case if divine mercy is to be perfect. Mercy that could forgive sin and yet let the sinner live in sin would be limited and superficial mercy. It would be unequal and deformed mercy. It would be mercy that is lame in one foot and paralyzed in one hand. Which do you think is the greater advantage, to be cleansed from the guilt of sin, or to be delivered from the power of sin? I will not attempt to debate such a question about two such outstanding mercies. Neither of them would be available to us except through the precious blood of Jesus. But it seems to me, if we are to compare them, that to be delivered from the power of sin, to be made holy, to be made like God, is the greater of the two.

To be forgiven is a favor too large to measure. We make this one of the first notes of our psalm of praise: "Who forgives all your iniquity." But if we could be forgiven, and were then allowed to love sin, to run wild in iniquity, and to wallow in lust, what would be the use of that kind of forgiveness? Might it not turn out to be a poisoned sweet that would effectively destroy us? To be washed, and yet lie in the mud; to be pronounced clean, and yet have the white mark of leprosy on one's face, would be mocking mercy. What good is it to bring someone out of their grave if you leave them dead? We thank God, that he who forgives our sins also heals our diseases. He who washes us from the stains of the past also lifts us out of the filthy ways of the present, and keeps us from failing in the future. We must accept with joy both repentance and forgiveness. They cannot be separated. The inheritance from God is one and cannot be split up. It is all or nothing. To divide the work of grace would be like King Solomon when he settled the dispute between the two women by saying, "Divide the living child in two, and give half to the one and half to the other."

Those who would permit this to happen have no interest in the outcome.

I will ask you who are seeking the Lord, whether you would be satisfied with only one of these mercies without the other. Would you be content, my reader, if God would forgive your sin and then allow you to be as worldly and wicked as before? No, no! The spirit that has been given new life is more afraid of sin itself than the punishment that results from it. The cry of your heart is not, "Who will deliver me from punishment?" but, "'Wretched man that I am! Who will deliver me from this body of death?' Who will give me the power to overcome temptation, and to become holy, even as God is holy?" Repentance and forgiveness go together to make up the gracious desire to be holy as God is holy. Both are necessary for salvation to be complete and to be holy. Rest assured that if you have one, you have both.

Repentance and forgiveness are joined together in the experience of all believers. There was never a person yet who sincerely repented of sin, with believing repentance, who was not forgiven. On the other hand, there was never a person forgiven who had not repented of their sin. I do not hesitate to say that there never has been, there is not now, and there never will be any case of sin being washed away, unless at the same time the heart was led to repentance and faith in Christ. Hatred of sin and a sense of pardon come into the soul together and stay together as long as we live.

Repentance and forgiveness act together and react together. Therefore, the person who is forgiven repents and the person who repents is forgiven. Remember that forgiveness leads to repentance, like we sing in Joseph Hart's hymn:

> Law and terrors do but harden,
>> All the while they work alone;
> But a sense of blood-bought pardon
>> Soon dissolves a heart of stone.

When we are certain that we are forgiven, then we hate sin. I suppose that when faith grows into complete assurance, when we are certain beyond a doubt that the blood of Jesus has washed us whiter than snow, it is then that repentance reaches its greatest height. As our faith grows, so does our repentance. Make no mistake; repentance is not something that lasts only for days or weeks. It is not a temporary penance to get over as soon as possible. No. Like faith, repentance is a grace that is given for a lifetime. God's little children repent and so do young adults and senior citizens in the family of God. Repentance is the inseparable companion of faith. We walk by faith, not by sight, and all the while the tear of repentance gleams in the eye of faith. True repentance comes from faith in Jesus and true faith in Jesus is always influenced by repentance. Faith and repentance are like conjoined twins that cannot be separated. To the degree that we believe in the forgiving love of Christ, to the same degree we repent. In proportion as we repent of sin and hate evil, in that proportion we rejoice in the fullness of pardon that Jesus is pleased to give. You will never value pardon unless you feel repentance. You will never experience the depths of repentance until you know that you are pardoned. It may seem strange, but it is really true. The bitterness of repentance and the sweetness of pardon blend to flavor every life of grace and bring happiness beyond compare.

These two covenant gifts each point to the other. If I know that I repent, then I know that I am forgiven. How am I to know that I am forgiven except that I also know that I have repented, that I have turned my back on my former sinful life? To be a believer is to be penitent. Faith and repentance are two spokes in the same wheel, two handles of the same plow. Repentance has been well described as a heart broken *for* sin and *from* sin. It may also be explained as a broken heart that is turning from sin and returning to the Father. It is a change of mind of the most thorough and radical kind. It results in sorrow for the past and a determination to change in the future.

> Repentance is to leave
> The sins we loved before;
> And show that we in earnest grieve,
> By doing so no more.

If this is the case in our life, then we may be certain that we are forgiven; because the Lord never caused a heart to be broken *for* sin and *from* sin, without pardoning it. If, on the other hand, we are enjoying pardon, through the blood of Jesus, and are justified by faith, and have peace with God through Jesus Christ our Lord, then we know that our repentance and faith are genuine.

Do not think of your repentance as the reason for your forgiveness, but as the companion of it. Do not expect to be able to repent until you see the grace of our Lord Jesus and his willingness to blot out your sin. Keep these blessed things in their proper places and see them in their relation to each other. They are like the two majestic pillars that Solomon had built at the entrance to the temple of the Lord; he named one Jachin and the other Boaz. Repentance is our Jachin and forgiveness is our Boaz that stand at the entrance of our pardon. No one comes to God correctly unless they pass between the pillars of repentance and forgiveness. The rainbow of covenant grace can be seen in all its beauty when the teardrops of repentance shine through the light of complete forgiveness. Repentance of sin and faith in divine pardon make up the foundation of true conversion. They are the signs of an Israelite in whom there is no deceit.

To come back to the Bible passage that we have been considering: both forgiveness and repentance flow from the same source and are given by the same Savior. The Lord Jesus in his glory gives both to the same people. Do not look for forgiveness or repentance anywhere else. Jesus has both ready, and is prepared to give them now, most freely to all who will accept them from him. Never forget that Jesus gives everything that is needed for our salvation. It is extremely important that all seekers after mercy remember this. Faith is as much the gift of God as is the Savior on whom that faith depends. Repenting for sin is as truly the work of grace as is Christ's atoning work on the cross by which sin is blotted out.

From beginning to end, salvation is by grace alone. Please do not misunderstand me. It is not the Holy Spirit who repents. He has never done anything for which he needs to repent. If he could repent, he could not repent for us. Each of us must repent for our own sin; otherwise we cannot be saved from the power of sin. It is not the Lord Jesus Christ who repents. Of what does he have to repent? We must do our own repenting with the full power of our mind. The will, the affections, the emotions, must all work together in the blessed work of repentance for sin. And yet at the back of everything that we do in repenting, there is a secret holy influence that melts the hearts, creates sorrow, and produces a complete change in us. The Spirit of God makes us aware of what sin is and makes it sickening in our eyes. The Spirit of God also turns us toward holiness, makes us wholeheartedly appreciate, love, and desire it, and drives us onward from one level of sanctification to another. The Spirit of God works in us, both to will and to work for God's good pleasure. Let us submit ourselves at once to the good Spirit, so that he may lead us to Jesus, who will freely give us the double blessing of repentance and forgiveness, according to the riches of his grace.

"For by grace you have been saved."

# CHAPTER SIXTEEN

# How Repentance Is Given

Let us now return to that grand text: "God exalted him at his right hand as Leader and Savior, to give repentance to Israel and forgiveness of sins." Our Lord Jesus Christ has ascended up into heaven so that grace may come down to us. His fame is used to give even more honor to his grace. The Lord has risen to heaven with the full intention of bringing believing sinners upward with him. He is honored to give repentance. We will realize this if we remember a few great truths.

The work that our Lord Jesus has done has made repentance *possible, available,* and *acceptable.* The law makes no mention of repentance. Rather, it plainly says, "The soul who sins shall die." What would your repenting or mine be worth if the Lord Jesus had not died and risen again and gone to the Father? We might feel deep regret and be terrified of God's wrath, but we would never feel true repentance with its hope of fellowship with God. As a natural feeling, repentance is nothing very special. It is usually so mixed with a selfish fear of punishment that very little merit is attached to it. If Jesus had not become involved and created a wealth of merit for us, our tears of repentance would be just so much water spilled on the ground. Jesus is exalted on high so that, through the strength of his pleading for us, our repentance may be accepted by God. Jesus made our repentance acceptable before God. Otherwise it would not be acceptable.

When Jesus was exalted on high, the Spirit of God was poured out to deliver the graces needed for our salvation. The Holy Spirit creates repentance in us by supernaturally changing our nature and taking away the heart of stone from our flesh. Do not sit down and try to force yourself to cry impossible tears. Repentance does not come from our unwilling nature. Repentance is the free gift of sovereign grace. Do not bother going to your room and trying to produce feelings that your heart of stone cannot manufacture. Instead, go to Mount Calvary and see how Jesus died. Lift up your eyes to the hills from where your help comes. The Spirit of God has come on purpose to change people's spirits and produce repentance in them, just as he once hovered over the empty earth and created life. Breathe your prayer to him, "Blessed Spirit, live within me. Make my heart tender and humble, so that I may hate sin and sincerely repent of it." He will hear your cry and answer you.

Remember, also, that when our Lord Jesus was exalted, he not only gave us repentance by sending the Holy Spirit, but he dedicated all creation and the secret workings of God to bring about our salvation. Any one of them may be used to bring us to repentance. He used the crow of a rooster to bring Peter to repentance. He used an earthquake to bring the jailer to repentance. Our Lord Jesus sits at the right hand of God, and rules all things here below, and makes them work together for the salvation of his redeemed. He uses both bitters and sweets, trials and joys, to cause sinners to turn to God. Be thankful to the God who made you poor, or sick, or sad, because Jesus uses all of these things to change your spirit and turn you to himself. The Lord's mercy often rides to the door of our hearts on the black horse of affliction. Jesus uses the whole range of our experience to wean us from earth and woo us to heaven. Christ is exalted to the throne of heaven and earth so that he can use all the powers at his disposal to graciously soften hard hearts through repentance.

God is also at work at this very hour in other ways. He whispers to your conscience, he speaks to you through his inspired Bible, by those of us who teach and preach from that Bible, and by praying friends with sincere and serious hearts. He can send a word to you that will strike your rocky heart, like Moses struck the rock with his rod, and caused streams of repentance to flow forth. He can bring to mind some heartbreaking text out of the Holy Bible that will conquer you immediately. He can mysteriously soften you and cause a holy frame of mind to come over you when you least expect it. Know this, Jesus reigns in the glorious splendor of his kingdom and has limitless ways of working repentance in those to whom he gives forgiveness. He is waiting even now to give repentance to you. Ask him for it at once.

Look and be encouraged by how the Lord Jesus Christ gives this repentance to the most unlikely people in the world. He is happy to give Israel repentance. To Israel! During the times when the apostles spoke, Israel was the nation that had sinned so terribly against light and love. They dared to say, "His blood be on us and on our children." Yet Jesus was pleased to give *them* repentance! What a marvel of grace! If you have been brought up in the brightest of Christian light, and yet have rejected it, there is still hope. If you have sinned against conscience, and against the Holy Spirit, and against the love of Jesus, there is still space for repentance. You may be as hard as unbelieving Israel of old, and yet softening may come to you, because Jesus will be honored and he has unlimited power to save you. For those who went the furthest in iniquity, and knowingly and intentionally sinned against God, the Lord Jesus is exalted to give them repentance and forgiveness of sins. I am happy to have such a full and wonderful gospel to proclaim to you. And you should be happy to be able to read about it!

The hearts of the children of Israel had grown as hard as solid rock. The reformer, Martin Luther, used to think it was impossible for a Jew to be converted. We are far from agreeing with him, and yet we must admit that the descendants of Israel have been exceptionably stubborn in their rejection of the Savior over these many centuries. Truly did the Lord say, "My people did not listen to my voice; Israel would not submit to me." "He came to his own, and his own people did not receive him." Yet our Lord Jesus is exalted because he gave repentance and forgiveness to Israel. My reader is probably a Gentile. But you may still have a very stubborn heart that has stood out against the Lord Jesus for many years. And yet our Lord can work repentance in you. Perhaps you will yet feel like William Hone did after he finally yielded to divine love. He was the author of those most entertaining volumes called *The Everyday Book*. But before that he had been a determined nonbeliever. After sovereign grace changed him, he wrote:

> The proudest heart that ever beat
>> Has been subdued in me;
> The wildest will that ever rose
>> To scorn your cause and help your foes
>> Is silenced my Lord, by you.
>
> Your will, and not my will be done,
>> My heart be ever yours;
> Confessing you the mighty Word,
>> My Savior Christ, my God, my Lord,
>> Your cross will be my sign.

The Lord can give repentance to the most unlikely people. He can turn lions into lambs and ravens into doves. Let us look to him for that great change to happen in us. Thinking about the death of Christ is one of the surest and quickest ways of achieving repentance. Do not try to pump up repentance from the dry well of your corrupt nature. It is contrary to all experience to suppose you can force your soul into a state of grace. Take your heart in prayer to him who understands it, and say, "Lord, cleanse my heart. Lord, renew it. Lord, work repentance in it." The more you try to produce emotions of repentance in yourself, the more you will be disappointed. But if you believe that Jesus died for you, and meditate on that, repentance will burst out. Think about the Lord shedding his heart's blood out of love to you. Picture in your mind the agony and bloody sweat, the cross and the suffering; and, as you do this, he who bore all this grief will look at you, and with that look he will do for you what he did for Peter, and you will also go out and weep bitterly. He who died for you can, by his gracious Spirit, make you die to sin. He who has gone to glory on your behalf can draw your soul after him, away from evil, and toward holiness.

I will be satisfied if I can leave this one thought with you: Do not look under the ice to find fire, do not depend on your own natural heart to find repentance. Look to the Living One for life. Look to Jesus for everything you need in this life and the next. Never look anywhere else for any part of that which Jesus loves to give. And remember, Christ is everything!

# CHAPTER SEVENTEEN

# The Fear of Losing Your Salvation

There is a fear that haunts the minds of many who are coming to Christ. They are afraid that they will not persevere or continue to the end. I have heard seekers say: "If I were to trust my soul to Jesus, yet I might go back to my old ways and end up being damned. I have experienced hopeful feelings before now and they have died away. My tendencies to do good have been like the morning cloud or as the early dew, that are gone before the morning is over. They have come quickly, lasted for a little while, seemed to promise much, and then vanished away."

I believe that this fear is often the father of the fact. There have been some who have been afraid to trust Christ forever. They failed because their faith was only temporary and was not enough to save them. They began by trusting in Jesus to some extent, but they looked to themselves to persevere and keep them on the road to heaven. They had set out with an imperfect view of faith and the natural result was that they turned back before long. If our trust to hold on is in ourselves, then we will not hold on. Even though we rest in Jesus for a part of our salvation, we will fail if we trust in ourselves for any part of it. No chain is stronger than its weakest link. If we hope in Jesus for everything except one thing, we will totally fail, because we will fail at that one point.

I have no doubt whatever that a mistake about the perseverance of the saints has prevented many from continuing in the faith who otherwise seemed to be growing in the Christian walk. What brought them to a stop? They trusted to themselves for that growing and so they stopped short of bearing fruit. Beware of mixing even a little of self into the cement with which you build, or you will weaken the mortar, and the bricks will not hold together. If you look to Christ for your beginnings, beware of looking to yourself for your endings. Jesus said, "I am the Alpha and the Omega, the first and the last, the beginning and the end." See to it that you make him your Omega as well as your Alpha. If you begin in the Spirit you must not hope to be made perfect by the flesh. Begin the way you intend to continue, and continue as you began, and let the Lord be your beginning and end and everything in between. Oh, that God the Holy Spirit may give us a very clear idea of where our strength to continue must come, the true power that will preserve us until the day of our Lord's appearing!

Here is what Paul once said on this subject when he was writing to the Corinthians:

"Our Lord Jesus Christ, who will sustain you to the end, guiltless in the day of our Lord Jesus Christ. God is faithful, by whom you were called into the fellowship of his Son, Jesus Christ our Lord" (1 Corinthians 1:7b-9).

Paul's words silently acknowledge a great need, by explaining to us how our need is provided for. Wherever the Lord supplies something, we can be quite certain there was a need for it, because the covenant of grace does not come with excess baggage. King Solomon made 200 large shields of beaten gold that were hung in his courts and never intended for actual combat, but there is no such thing in the arsenal of God. We are certain to need everything God has provided. Between now and that last great day, every promise of God and everything he has provided for the covenant of grace will be required. The urgent need of the believing soul is evidence of God's care and proof of his love. His care provides divine strength to continue and his love protects us to the end.

Even the most advanced believers find this necessary. When Paul wrote to the saints at Corinth, he was writing to people who had been Christians a long time, who were advanced in their faith. He said, "I give thanks to my God always for you because of the grace of God that was given you in Christ Jesus," and "that in every way you were enriched in him." Yet he went right on to say, "Our Lord Jesus Christ, who *will sustain* you to the end." These people are the very ones who most certainly feel the need of new grace every day if they are to hold on, and hold out, and come off as conquerors at the end. If you were not saints you would have no grace and you would not feel the need for more grace. But because you are men and women of God, you are deeply aware that the demands of the spiritual life need new grace every day. The marble statue needs no food, but the living person hungers and thirsts. They rejoice that their bread and water are provided for them. Otherwise they would certainly faint along the way. The believer's personal needs require that they draw daily from the great source of all supplies. What could they do if they could not go to their God?

This is true of the most gifted of the saints. The believers at Corinth "were enriched in [Jesus] in all speech and all knowledge," and yet they needed gracious strength to the end, otherwise their gifts and accomplishments would prove their ruin. If we had "the tongues of men and of angels," but did not receive fresh grace, where would we be? If we gained experience until we were fathers and mothers in the church, if we had been taught by God to the point we had prophetic powers, and understood all mysteries, and had all knowledge we still could not live a single day without the divine life flowing into us from our Covenant Head. How could we hope to hold on for a single hour, to say nothing of a lifetime, unless the Lord holds us throughout? He who began the good work in us must be the one to bring it to completion at the day of Jesus Christ or it will prove a painful failure.

This need for daily grace proceeds very much from our own actions. Some have a painful fear that they will not continue in grace because they know how fickle they are. They are naturally unsteady and prone to change. Some people naturally hold to their traditions and values even to the point of stubbornness, but others are just as naturally changeable and unpredictable. Like butterflies they flit from flower to flower, until they visit all the beauties of the garden, and stay on none of them. They never stay long enough in one place to do any good; not even in their job or intellectual pursuits. This type of person may well be afraid that ten, twenty, thirty, forty, perhaps fifty years of carefully walking with the Lord will be more than they can handle. We see people joining first one church and then another, until they could give details of every denomination imaginable. They try everything for a short time and nothing for long. These people have a double need to pray that they may be divinely strengthened and be made not only committed but unmovable. Otherwise they will not be found "always abounding in the work of the Lord."

All of us, even if we have no natural tendency to fickleness, must feel our own weakness if we are really born again of God. Dear reader, do you not find enough in any one single day to make you stumble? I trust you have that desire to walk in perfect holiness, that you have a high standard of what a Christian should be. But do you not find that before the breakfast table is cleared, you have already displayed enough folly to make you ashamed of yourself? If we were to live alone like a hermit, temptation would follow us; because as long as we cannot escape from ourselves we cannot escape the temptations to sin. There is within our hearts that which should make us watchful and humble before God. If he does not give us strength, we are so weak that we will stumble and fall, not defeated by an enemy, but by our own carelessness. Lord, be our strength, because we are weakness itself.

Besides that, there is the weariness that comes from a long life. When we begin our new Christian life we mount up with wings like eagles, later we run and are not weary. In our best and truest days we walk and do not faint. Our pace seems slower, but it is more functional and stable. I pray to God that the energy of our youth may continue, as long as it is the energy of the Holy Spirit and not the mere activity of proud flesh. The person who has been on the road to heaven for a long time discovers that the road is rough and there was a good reason why the Lord promised the Israelites in the wilderness that their shoes would not wear out. Like Christian in *The Pilgrim's Progress*, they have discovered that there are Hills of Difficulty and Valleys of Humiliation; that there is the Valley of the Shadow of Death, and, worse still, a Vanity Fair. The road to the Promised Land passes near these. If there are to be Delectable Mountains (and, thank God, there are), there are also Castles of Despair, inside of which pilgrims are too often found. All things considered, it is no great wonder that those who continue on the path of holiness to the end are looked on as remarkable.

We say, with Bunyan's Christian, "Oh world of wonders, I can say no less. That I should be preserved in that distress." The days of a Christian's life are like so many diamonds of mercy threaded on the golden string of divine faithfulness. In heaven we will tell angels, and rulers, and authorities, and cosmic powers about how the unsearchable riches of Christ were spent on us, and enjoyed by us while we were here below. We have been on the brink of death and kept alive. Our spiritual life has been a flame burning in the midst of the sea, a stone floating on air. It will amaze the universe to see us enter the pearly gate, blameless in the day of our Lord Jesus Christ. We should be overwhelmed with grateful wonder if the Lord keeps us for even an hour. I trust we are.

As if our natural temperaments, and aging, and the temptations of this life were not enough concerns to worry over, there are far more. We have to think of the world we live in. To many of God's people it is a howling wilderness. Some of us are greatly blessed with material things, but others have a hard go of it. Some of us begin our day with prayer and the sounds of holy song often fill our homes. But many good people have hardly risen from their knees in the morning before they are greeted with blasphemy. They go to work, and all day long they are tormented, like righteous Lot in Sodom, by the lawless deeds they see and hear. Can you even walk in the public streets without your ears being afflicted with foul language? The world is no friend to grace. We live in an enemy's country. The best we can do with this world is to get through it as quickly as we can. A robber lurks behind every bush. We need to travel everywhere with a "drawn sword" in our hand, or at least with that weapon which is All-Prayer always at our side. We have to contend for every inch of our way. Make no mistake about this or you are in for a rude awakening from your fond delusion. Oh God, help us, and strengthen us to the end, or where will we be?

True religion is supernatural at its beginning, supernatural throughout life, and supernatural at its close. It is the work of God from first to last. There is a great need for the hand of the Lord to be stretched out even today. My reader is feeling that need now and I am glad they are, because that will mean they will look to the Lord for their strength, the Lord who alone is able to keep us from failing and to glorify us with his Son.

# CHAPTER EIGHTEEN

# How Can I Continue On?

I want you to notice the security that Paul confidently expected for all Christians. Our Lord Jesus Christ "will sustain you to the end, guiltless in the day of our Lord Jesus Christ." That word "sustain" can be difficult to get our arms around. Some translations use the word "confirm." We have heard that word used to describe someone who is very committed to a lifestyle. A *confirmed* bachelor is a man who is committed to not being married. Some have used the term to describe awful habits of sin and error. Think of a confirmed drunkard, or a confirmed thief, or a confirmed liar. It would be terrible for someone to be confirmed in unbelief and ungodliness.

Paul is stating that you will be a confirmed Christian to the end. Our Lord Jesus Christ will keep you steadfast, loyal, faithful and devoted to him to the end of your natural life. He will uphold you and supply you with the strength and support to carry on to the end. This is divine confirmation! It can only be enjoyed by those who have already shown that they have received the grace of God. It is the work of the Holy Spirit. He gives faith and he sustains it; that is, he strengthens faith and makes it permanent. He kindles love in us, protects it, and increases its flame. He who began a good work in you will teach you by the Holy Spirit to grow in grace and reach higher levels of clearness and certainty. Holy actions are sustained or confirmed in us until they become habits. Holy feelings are sustained until they become a pattern in our lives. Experience and practice confirm our beliefs and our goals. Our joys and our sorrows are used to confirm us. Our successes and our failures become holy ways to sustain us. Our faith is like the tree whose roots grow deep and strong through both soft showers and rough winds. The mind is instructed and as it gains knowledge it multiplies reasons for staying on the good path. The heart is comforted and so it clings more tightly to the comforting truth. The grip grows stronger, and the step grows firmer, and the Christian becomes more solid and true.

Most people tend to naturally grow and mature, but growing in grace is the work of the Holy Spirit. It is as much his work as our conversion was. The Lord will most certainly give it to those who are relying on him for eternal life. He works within us to deliver us from being as "unstable as water," and causes us to be rooted and grounded. This building us up into Christ Jesus and causing us to follow him is a part of the way he saves us. Dear reader, you may look for this sustaining every day and you will not be disappointed. Christ, in whom you trust, will make you "like a tree planted by streams of water that yields its fruit in its season." You will be sustained so that your "leaf does not wither."

A confirmed Christian is a great strength to a church. He or she is a comfort to those who are sorrowing and a help to the weak. Would you not like to be one? Confirmed believers are pillars in the house of our God. They are not carried about by every wind of doctrine nor brought down by sudden temptation. They are a tower of strength to others and act as anchors in the time of church trouble. You who are beginning the holy life hardly dare to hope that you will become like them. But do not fear. The good Lord will do the same work in you that he has in them. You who are "newborn infants" in Christ will one day be called a "father" or "mother" in the church. Hope for this great thing; but hope for it as a gift of grace, and not as a reward for your work, or as the result of your own zeal.

The inspired apostle Paul spoke of these people as being sustained to the end. He expected that the grace of God would be with them and preserve them to the end of their lives or until the Lord Jesus would come. In fact, he expected that the entire church of God in every place and in all time would be kept to the end of this dispensation, until the

Lord Jesus would come as the Bridegroom to celebrate the wedding feast with his perfected Bride. Everyone who is in Christ will be sustained in him until that glorious day. Has Jesus not said, "Because I live, you also will live"? He also said, "I give [my sheep] eternal life, and they will never perish, and no one will snatch them out of my hand." He who began a good work in you will bring it to completion at the day of Jesus Christ. The work of grace in the soul is not a superficial change. The life implanted as the new birth comes from a living and indestructible seed through the living and abiding word of God that remains forever. The promises God made to believers are not temporary and they include the promise that believers will be sustained until they reach endless glory. We are kept by the power of God, through faith to salvation. "The righteous holds to his way, and he who has clean hands grows stronger and stronger." This is not the result of our own excellence or strength, but it is a gift of free and undeserved favor for those who believe "and are kept by Jesus Christ." There will be one flock, and there is one Shepherd, and Jesus will lose none of his sheep. No member of his body will die. No jewel will be missing in the day when he makes up his treasured possession. Dear reader, the salvation that is received by faith is not something that lasts only for months or years. Our Lord Jesus secured "an eternal redemption" for us and that which is "eternal" cannot come to an end.

Paul also declared his belief that the saints in Corinth would be sustained "to the end," guiltless in the day of our Lord Jesus Christ. This having no guilt is a precious part of our being confirmed. To be kept holy is better than merely to be kept safe. It is a dreadful thing when you see religious people stumbling out of one dishonorable thing only to step into another. They have not believed in the power of our Lord to make them blameless. The lives of some professing Christians are a series of stumbles; they are never quite down, and yet they are seldom on their feet. This is not appropriate for a believer. Believers are invited to walk with God, and by faith they can reach a steady walk in holiness, as they should. The Lord is able, not only to save us from hell, but to keep us from falling. We do not need to yield to temptation. Is it not written, "Sin will have no dominion over you"? The Lord is able to guard the feet of his faithful ones. He will do it if we trust him to. We do not need to allow our garments to become unclean, we may by his grace keep them pure and undefiled before God. We are obligated to do this, because without holiness "no one will see the Lord."

The apostle predicted something for these believers in Corinth that he wanted all of us to desire; that we may be preserved, that we would be "guiltless in the day of our Lord Jesus Christ." That word "guiltless" has also been translated "blameless." A better word might be "unimpeachable." May God grant that we stand free from all charges in that last great day; that no one in the whole universe may dare to challenge our claim to be the redeemed by the Lord. We have sins and weaknesses to mourn over, but these are not the kind of faults that would prove us to be outside of Christ. We will be clear of hypocrisy, deceit, hatred, and delight in sin—these would be fatal charges. In spite of our failings, the Holy Spirit can work in us a character that is spotless before others; so that, like Daniel, the only thing about which their accusing tongues will have to complain is our religion. Multitudes of godly men and women have displayed lives so transparent and so consistent that no one could argue the point. The Lord will be able to say about many believers, as he did about Job when Satan stood before him, "Have you considered my servant Job, that there is none like him on the earth, a blameless and upright man, who fears God and turns away from evil?" This is what my reader must look for from the Lord. This is the victory of the saints—to continue to follow the Lamb wherever he goes, while maintaining our integrity as before the loving God. May we never turn aside into crooked ways and give our enemies reason to blaspheme. The apostle John tells us that true believers protect themselves "and the evil one does not touch him." May this be written about us!

My friend, who is just beginning the divine life, the Lord can give you a blameless character. You may have gone far into sin in your past life, but the Lord can thoroughly deliver you from the power of your former habits, and make you an example of virtue. Not only can he make you moral, but he can make you hate every false way and follow after all that is godly. Do not doubt it. The foremost of sinners do not need to be even a step behind the purest saints. Believe this, and according to your faith it will done to you.

Oh, what joy it will be to be found blameless in the day of judgment! We can join in honestly singing that charming hymn;

> Bold will I stand in that great day,
>> For who can anything to my charge lay;
> While through Your blood acquitted I am,
>> From sin's tremendous curse and shame?

What a joy it will be, when heaven and earth will pass away, to face the Judge of all with fearless courage! This joy will be shared by everyone who looks alone to the grace of God in Christ Jesus who wages truly holy war with all sin.

# CHAPTER NINETEEN

# Why Believers Persevere

We saw in the last chapter that Paul believed that believers would remain confirmed Christians to the end. This hope filled Paul's heart regarding the believers in Corinth and continues to give comfort to those who tremble about their future. But why was it that he believed that the brothers and sisters in Corinth would be sustained to the end?

Paul actually included the reasons in the passage we have already quoted:

"God is faithful, by whom you were called into the fellowship of his Son, Jesus Christ our Lord" (1 Corinthians 1:9).

The apostle does not say, "*You* are faithful." Sadly, the faithfulness of humans is not very reliable, nor worth much. He does not say, "You have faithful pastors to lead and guide you and therefore I trust you will be safe." Oh, no! If we are kept by the power of other people we will not be safe. Paul says, "God is faithful." If we continue faithful to the end, it will be because God is faithful. The whole weight of our salvation must rest on the faithfulness of our covenant God. We are as changing as the wind, as easily broken as a spider's web, and our "knees turn to water". We cannot depend on our natural abilities or our spiritual accomplishments. We must depend on God, because *he* "remains faithful."

He is faithful in his love. He is "the Father of lights with whom there is no variation or shadow due to change." He is faithful to his intentions. He does not start a work in someone and then leave it unfinished. He is faithful in his relationships. As a Father he will not abandon his children, as a friend he will not reject his people, and as a Creator he will not give up on the work of his own hands. He is faithful to his promises. He will never break even one of them to any believer. He is faithful to his covenant that he made with us in Christ Jesus, and accepted by the blood of Jesus' sacrifice. He is faithful to his Son. He will not allow his precious blood to be spilled in vain. He is faithful to his people to whom he has promised eternal life. He will not turn away from them.

God's faithfulness is the foundation and cornerstone of our hope of persevering to the end. The saints will persevere in holiness, because God perseveres in grace. God continues to bless and therefore believers continue to be blessed. He continues to sustain his people and therefore his people continue to keep his commandments. This is good solid ground to rest on and it is delightfully well suited as the title of this little book, *All of Grace*. Free kindness and infinite mercy ring in the dawn of salvation, and the same sweet bells ring the same pleasant tune throughout our entire lives of grace.

Do you see that the only reasons for hoping that we will be sustained to the end, and be found guiltless at the last, are found in our God? And in him these reasons are extremely plentiful.

First, they can be seen in what God has done. He has gone so far in blessing us that it is not possible for him to turn back. Paul reminds us that he has called us "into the fellowship of his Son, Jesus Christ our Lord." Is he the one who has called us? Then it is a call that cannot be reversed, because "the gifts and the calling of God are irrevocable." God's works are effectual; that is, they always succeed. The effectual call of his grace cannot be overturned. "Those whom he called he also justified, and those whom he justified he also glorified." This is the unchanging rule of divine policy.

There is a common call, of which it is said, "Many are called, but few are chosen," but this is another kind of call. It is the call of special love and involves the recipient responding to it. It is the same as the call to Abraham's offspring, of whom the Lord said, I took you "from the ends of the earth, and called from its farthest corners, saying to you, 'You are my servant, I have chosen you and not cast you off.'"

We see strong reasons for our preservation and future glory in what the Lord has done, because the Lord has called us *into the fellowship of his Son Jesus Christ.* That means we have entered into a partnership with Jesus Christ. I would ask you to carefully consider what this means. If you have truly been called by divine grace, you have entered into fellowship with the Lord Jesus Christ in such a way that you have actually become a joint-owner with him in all things. From now on the Most High God sees you as being one with Jesus. The Lord Jesus bore your sins in his own body on the cross, he became a curse for you; and at the same time he became your righteousness, and you have been justified in him. You are Christ's and Christ is yours. As Adam stood in the place of all of his descendants, so does Jesus stand in the place of all who are in him. Those who are united to Jesus by faith are one like a husband and wife are one. It is a marriage that can never end in divorce.

But it is even more than that. Believers are part of Christ's body. They are joined to him and have become one in a loving, living way. God has called us into this marriage, this fellowship, this partnership. He has given us this sign and promise that he will sustain us to the end. If we were looked at as separate from Christ, we would be poor perishable souls, soon destroyed and carried away to destruction. But because we have been made one with Jesus we have "become partakers of the divine nature" and supplied with his immortal life. Our destiny has been linked with our Lord's and until *he* can be destroyed it is not possible for us to perish.

Give this partnership with the Son of God a lot of thought. You have been called into this relationship and all of your hope lies in it. You can never be poor while Jesus is rich, because you are partners in the same company. You can never be troubled with a lack of anything, because you are a joint owner with the Lord who owns heaven and earth. You can never fail. If one of the partners in the company is as poor as a church mouse, and is completely bankrupt, and cannot even begin to pay even a small amount of their heavy debts, yet the other partner is inconceivably, inexhaustibly rich. With a partnership like

104 | All of Grace

that, you are raised above the misery of today, the changes of the future, and the shock of the end of all things. The Lord has called you into the fellowship of his Son Jesus Christ and by that action he has put you into the place of perfect safety.

If you are truly a believer, you are one with Jesus, and you are safe. Can you not see that this must be the case? If you have been made one with Jesus by the irreversible act of God, then you must be sustained until the day of his appearing. Christ and the believing sinner are in the same boat. The believer will never drown unless Jesus sinks with them. The connection between Jesus and his redeemed ones is such that he himself must be struck down, overcome, and dishonored, before the least of his purchased ones can be injured. His name is at the head of the company. Until it can be dishonored there is no reason for us to be anxious about failing.

We are eternally linked with Jesus. So, then, let us go forward into the unknown future with the utmost confidence. If the world should sneer at us and cry, "Who is that coming up from the wilderness, leaning on her beloved?" we will joyfully admit that we do lean on Jesus, and that we intend to lean on him more and more. Our faithful God is a well of delight that will not run dry and our fellowship with the Son of God is an ever-flowing river of joy. We cannot know these glorious things and be discouraged. Instead we proclaim with the apostle, "Who shall separate us from the love of Christ?"

# CHAPTER TWENTY

# In Closing

If my reader has not accepted what I have put forward in these pages, I am truly sorry. Reading a book is of small value unless the truths it contains are understood, taken to heart, and put into practice. It is like seeing lots of food in a store and yet remaining hungry, because it was not taken home and eaten. Dear reader, it is all pointless that you and I have met, unless you have actually taken hold of Christ Jesus, my Lord. My desire in writing was definitely to benefit you and I have done my best to do so. It pains me if I have not been able to do you good, because I wanted to win that privilege. I was thinking of you when I wrote this page, and I set my pen down and bowed my knee in prayer for everyone who would read it. It is my firm conviction that great numbers of readers will get a blessing, even though *you* refuse to be included in that number. But why should *you* refuse?

If you have no desire for the wonderful blessing that I wanted to bring to you, at least do the right thing and admit that the blame for your final doom will not lie at my door. When the two of us meet before the great white throne you will not be able to accuse me of wasting the time you used, which you were kind enough to honor me with while you were reading my little book. God knows I wrote each line for your eternal good. Now in spirit I take you by the hand. I give you a firm grip. Do you feel my brotherly grasp? The tears are in my eyes as I look at you and say, "Why will you die? Do you refuse to think about your eternal soul? Will you perish through sheer carelessness? Oh, please do not do so. Weigh these serious matters. Your eternal future hangs in the balance. Do not refuse Jesus. Do not refuse his love, his blood, his salvation. Why would you? How can you? I plead with you; do not turn away from your Redeemer!"

On the other hand, if my prayers are heard, and you, my reader, have been led to trust the Lord Jesus and have received his salvation by grace, then always keep to this teaching and this way of living. Let Jesus be your all in all and let free grace be the one path by which you walk and advance. There is no life like the one that is lived under the smile of God. To receive everything as a free gift keeps the mind from self-righteous pride and from self-accusing despair. It makes the heart grow warm with grateful love. And this creates a feeling in the soul that is infinitely more acceptable to God than anything that can possibly come from slavish fear.

Those who hope to be saved by trying to do their best know nothing of that glowing enthusiasm, that holy warmth, that reverent joy in God, that comes with salvation freely given by the grace of God. The slavish spirit of saving ourselves is no match for the joyous spirit of knowing God has adopted us. The smallest response of faith has more virtue in it than all the struggles of trying to keep the law, or all the weary efforts of those who expect to climb to heaven by round after round of ceremonies. Faith is spiritual and that is why God, who is a spirit, delights in it. Years of saying prayers, and attending a church or chapel, and ceremonies, and going through the motions of worship, may only be an abomination in the sight of Almighty God. But even a glance from the eye of true faith is spiritual and therefore it is dear to him. "The Father is seeking such people to worship him." Look to the inner self first, to the spiritual person that you are, and the rest will follow in due time.

If you are saved, then be on the watch for the souls of others. Your own heart will not prosper unless it is filled with an intense concern to see others also blessed. The life of your soul depends on faith; its health depends on love. The person who does not ache to lead others to Jesus has never been under the spell of divine love. Get to the work of the Lord; get to the work of love. Begin at home. Next, visit your neighbors. Open the eyes of the street where you reside and the town where you live. Scatter the word of the Lord wherever you can.

Reader, meet me in heaven! Do not go down to hell. There is no coming back again from that place of misery. Why do you wish to enter the way of death when the gate of heaven is open before you? Do not refuse God's free pardon, his full salvation that Jesus gives to all who trust him. Do not hesitate, do not delay. You have had enough time to think about it, take action. Believe in Jesus now, settle the issue immediately. "Take with you words and return to the Lord. Say to him, 'Take away all iniquity.'" Do it this day. Remember, dear soul, it may be now or never with you. Make it now. It would be horrible if it were never.

I plead with you again, meet me in heaven.

Made in the USA
Middletown, DE
14 April 2022

64268433R00068